# Biblical Answers
## to Personal Problems

## Books in the Stephen F. Olford Biblical Preaching Library

*Biblical Answers to Personal Problems*
*Committed to Christ and His Church*
*Fresh Lessons from Former Leaders*
*The Pulpit and the Christian Calendar 1*
*The Pulpit and the Christian Calendar 2*
*The Pulpit and the Christian Calendar 3*
*Believing Our Beliefs*
*Living Words and Loving Deeds*

# Biblical Answers to Personal Problems

### Expounding Scripture's Relevance and Reality

## Stephen F. Olford

**BAKER BOOK HOUSE**
Grand Rapids, Michigan 49516

The following copyright owners have given permission to use excerpts from their material in the Stephen Olford Biblical Preaching Library:

# Contents

Introduction    7
1.  The Answer to Anxiety (Phil. 4:6–7)    11
2.  The Answer to Self-Esteem (Mark 12:30–31)    21
3.  The Answer to Care (1 Peter 5:6–11)    29
4.  The Answer to Guilt (1 John 1:1–7)    37
5.  The Answer to Loneliness (Ps. 68:5–6)    45
6.  The Answer to Hopelessness (1 Peter 3:13–16)    53
7.  The Answer to Suffering (2 Cor. 12:7–10)    61
8.  The Answer to Fearfulness (1 John 4:11–18)    69
9.  The Answer to Temptation (1 Cor. 10:6–13)    77
10. The Answer to Indecision (1 Kings 18:17–40)    87
11. The Answer to Despair (Deut. 33:26–29)    97
12. The Answer to Death (Heb. 9:24–28)    107
    Endnotes    115
    For Further Reading    119

# Introduction

I t has often been said that "our problems are not in Christianity, but in Christians!" As long as we have *people* we will have *problems*. This should not constitute an obstacle in our preaching, but rather an opportunity to show the reality and relevance of the living Word. The Bible solves problems that perplex. This is one of the great joys of expounding the Scriptures under the anointing of the Holy Spirit. It is the divine Counselor's function to ". . . guide [us] into all truth . . ." (John 16:13).

But now a word about the use of the expository sermon outlines that are featured in this first volume of the Stephen Olford Biblical Preaching Library.

For years my sermon outlines were personal and precious—a growing but private treasury of tested biblical messages. However, the constant pressures of my colleagues in the ministry—and especially the younger men who have asked for help—have persuaded me to make them available. My records also show that during my fourteen years at Calvary Baptist Church, New York City, preachers made up the greatest proportion of those who requested my weekly sermon outlines.

Further research has led me to concur with E. P. Alldredge, author of *101 Expository Sermon Outlines,* that "there are at least five . . . good reasons for the publication of sermon outlines and suggestions:

1. *Larger Help and Service:* Students of the Word of God, whether mature or immature, are helped more by studying the thought of another preacher's sermons than by studying his phraseology, though both are quite necessary—for the young preacher in particular.

2. *Great Timesaver:* One can read a volume of 100 sermon outlines in the same time that would be required for him to read a volume of ten sermons, written out in full. Let him do both, at least one a month if he would be a better preacher.

3. *Better Teaching Power:* Very few of the great teachers and professors in our colleges and theological schools bring the full texts of their lectures to their classes. Perhaps 95 percent of all the lectures thus given are presented to the students in the form of outlines. Sermon outlines follow this teaching method and undoubtedly have a greater teaching force in the minds of average students than the study of a few sermons in full text.

4. *Materials for the Unprepared Man:* We have to bear in mind, for instance, that approximately forty percent of a large denomination's ministers are without full college and seminary training. Perhaps one-third of them have had little college and no seminary training at all, unless it be a correspondence course. They need help and suggestions, need them constantly. Moreover, a large number of college and seminary trained preachers have real difficulty in outlining their sermons. If one can help these large groups with a section on sermon outlines, he is certainly doing God's service.

5. *All Too Few Expository Preachers:* A series of sermon outlines may revolutionize a preacher's study of the Bible and his plans for sermon building. Nothing could happen to ministers that would be of greater moment than the turning of their minds back to the Book itself and a real revival of expository preaching."[1]

For these five reasons and more, I commend my expository sermon outlines to pastors, seminarians, lay preachers and teachers "for the equipping of the saints for the work of ministry, for the edifying of the body of Christ" (Eph. 4:12). So I exhort you to "Preach the word! . . . [and] do the work of an evangelist" (2 Tim. 4:2, 5).

Stephen F. Olford

# 1

# The Answer to Anxiety
## *Philippians 4:6–7*

"Be anxious for nothing, but in everything by prayer and supplication, with thanksgiving, let your requests be made known to God" (4:6).

## Introduction

In his volume, *The Christian's Handbook of Psychiatry,* Dr. O. Quentin Hyder points out that there are probably more theories about the causes of anxiety than about any other diagnosis in the whole field of medicine. Several schools of thought have tried to dominate psychiatry over the last fifty years, and most of their differences are in the area of the origin and treatment of anxiety. No one has all the answers, but every theory is at least a partial explanation to the problem of the whole. While we thank God for human skills that have been developed to tackle this distressing condition, it is a wonderful comfort to know that the ultimate answer lies with God.

Of the many passages of Scripture to which we might turn in dealing with this subject, I know of no more relevant verses than Paul's words to the church at Philippi, where he says: "Be anxious for nothing, but in everything by prayer and supplication, with thanksgiving, let your requests be made known to God; and the peace of God, which surpasses all understanding, will guard your hearts and minds through Christ Jesus" (4:6–7). In simple terms, he gives us here God's answer to anxiety. There are three antidotes to this problem which are clearly suggested:

## I. There Must Be the Mastery of a Life of Prayer

"Be anxious for nothing (or be not overanxious about anything), but in everything by prayer and supplication, with thanksgiving, let your requests be made known to God" (4:6).

The story is told how the celebrated Austrian composer, Franz Joseph Haydn, was in a company of distinguished guests. The conversation turned to the best means of restoring mental energies when exhausted with long and difficult studies. One person said that his recourse was to drink a bottle of wine. Another remarked that his solution was to involve himself in the company of others. But when Haydn was asked what he would do he replied that his practice was to retire to his study and engage in prayer. Nothing, he explained, exerted a more happy and efficacious influence on his heart and mind than the power of prayer.

**Illustration**

Someone has well written of the change which comes about through the power of prayer:

Lord, what a change within us one short hour
Spent in Thy Presence will prevail to make!
What heavy burdens from our bosoms take!

What parched grounds refresh as with a shower!
We kneel and all around us seems to lower,
We rise, and all, the distant and the near,
Stands forth in sunny outline, bright and clear.
We kneel how weak, we rise how full of power!
Why therefore should we do ourselves this wrong,
Or others, that we are not always strong,
That we are ever overborne with care,
That we should ever weak or heartless be,
Anxious or troubled, when with us is prayer,
And joy and strength and courage are with Thee.[1]

It is important at this point, however, to observe that the mastery of a life of prayer is determined by two essential conditions:

## A. A Relationship to God

". . . in everything by prayer and supplication . . . through Christ Jesus" (4:6–7). No one can really pray unless he knows the way. The Lord Jesus declared, ". . . I am the way, the truth, and the life. No one comes to the Father except through Me" (John 14:6). Paul reminds us that ". . . there is one God and one Mediator between God and men, the Man Christ Jesus" (1 Tim. 2:5). We can never look up to heaven and say "Father" unless we have the witness of the Spirit in our hearts that we are children through faith in our Lord Jesus Christ (see Rom 8:16). This new birth into the family of God comes only through faith in Christ. John says, "But as many as received Him, to them He gave the right to become children of God, even to those who believe in His name: who were born, not of blood, nor of the will of the flesh, nor of the will of man, but of God" (John 1:12–13).

### Illustration

There was a godly man in Germany named Bengel, who was noted for his intimacy with Christ. A friend desired to watch the saintly man at his devotions, so he concealed himself one night in his room. Bengel sat long at his table, reading his New Testament. The hours passed. At length the clock struck midnight, and the old man spread out his hands and said with great joy, "Dear Lord Jesus, we are on the same old terms." Then closing his book, he was soon in bed and asleep. He had learned the secret of friendship with Christ.[2]

## B. A Reliance on God

". . . in everything by prayer and supplication . . . through Christ Jesus" (4:6–7). With that initial relationship there must be a continual reliance. The Bible reminds us that ". . . he who comes to God must believe that He is, and that He is a rewarder of those who diligently seek Him" (Heb. 11:6); and again: ". . . without faith it is impossible to please [God]" (Heb. 11:6). Jesus underscored this same truth when he said, ". . . whatever you ask in prayer, believing, you will receive" (Matt. 21:22). The mastery of prayer involves a childlike trust in a heavenly Father who knows, who loves, and cares. Like Haydn, let us daily prove the happy and efficacious influence of prayer in our lives. Paul says that this is an answer to the problem of anxiety.

### Illustration

J. Hudson Taylor served a lifetime as pioneer missionary in the interior of China. He was a man of inexhaustible energy, gentle patience, and spiritual stature. What was the secret of his power and goodness? People described him as totally dependent on the Lord. Those around him said: "He drew from the Bank of Heaven every farthing of his daily income. . . . Nothing ruffled his spirit. The serenity of the Lord Jesus Christ concerning any matter at any moment, this was his ideal and practical possession. . . . He knew there was a peace passing all understanding, and that he could not do without it."[3]

## II. There Must Be the Therapy of a Life of Peace

"Be anxious for nothing, but in everything by prayer and supplication, with thanksgiving, let your requests be made known to God; and the peace of God, which surpasses all understanding, will guard your hearts and minds through Christ Jesus" (4:6–7). When we come to know God as our Father, through faith in Jesus Christ, we experience at once what the Bible calls ". . . peace *with* God . . ." (Rom. 5:1). This is the peace of reconciliation. But what the apostle is describing in our text is something more: it is ". . . the peace *of* God . . ." (4:7) which keeps the heart and mind. That word *keep* is one of the strongest terms used in the New Testament to describe a garrison, or an army of sentinels.

Anxiety, for the most part, is created by the fears, frets, and frustrations that assail us from the world, the flesh, and the devil. But here is the promise of a peace which keeps us, and the effect of this peace is a God-given therapy.

### A. The Peace of God Stabilizes the Heart

". . . the peace of God . . . will guard your hearts" (4:7). The heart (cardia) signifies the hidden springs of our emotional life. How many people are emotionally disturbed because of anxiety! Indeed, most psychological and pathological problems can be traced to nervous tensions and emotional disturbances.

How wonderful to know that our hearts can be stabilized in the Lord when we come to God and receive his gift of peace. The hymnwriter expresses it perfectly:

> O what peace we often forfeit,
> O what needless pain we bear,
> All because we do not carry
> Everything to God in prayer!
>
> Joseph Scriven

Before Jesus left for heaven he declared: "Peace I leave with you, My peace I give to you; not as the world gives do I give to you. Let not your heart be troubled, neither let it be afraid" (John 14:27).

### B. The Peace of God Tranquilizes the Mind

". . . the peace of God . . . will guard your . . . minds . . ." (4:7). Paul could have easily been thinking of those glorious words from the Book of Isaiah where the prophet says, "You will keep him in perfect peace, Whose mind is stayed on You . . ." (Isa. 26:3). One of the sure tests of our having prevailed in prayer is the peace of mind which follows. The person who rises from his knees with annoying anxieties has not really prayed. Peace does not mean a retreat from the world, but rather a tranquility which comes and remains, though the outside world may be in turmoil. This is a peace which passes human understanding and is one of the glorious gifts of our God. Christ does not promise deliverance out of, or preservation from, calamities, but he does promise great peace of mind in the midst of them.

#### Illustration

Several years ago a submarine was being tested and had to remain submerged for many hours. When it returned to the harbor, the captain was asked, "How did the terrible storm last night affect you?" The officer looked at him in surprise and exclaimed, "Storm? We didn't even know there was one!" The sub had been so far beneath the surface that it had reached the area known to sailors as "the cushion of the sea." Although the ocean may be whipped into huge waves by high winds, the waters below are never stirred. A. T. Pierson said, "The peace of God is that eternal calm which lies far too deep in the praying, trusting soul to be reached by any external disturbances."[4]

## III. There Must Be the Victory of a Life of Praise

"Be anxious for nothing, but in everything by prayer and supplication, *with thanksgiving,* let your requests be made known to God" (4:6). The evidence of a peaceful heart and mind is a praising life. One of the chief causes of anxiety is preoccupation with our own particular problems. We cannot be caught up in this kind of introspection and be praiseful at one and the same time. This victory of a life of praise has two elements in it:

### A. A Trustfulness in God

". . . let your requests be made known to God" (4:6). There is no point in bringing requests to God if we do not believe that he is going to answer. This is why James says, "If any of you lacks wisdom, let him ask of God, who gives to all liberally and without reproach, and it will be given to him. But let him ask in faith, with no doubting, for he who doubts is like a wave of the sea driven and tossed by the wind" (James 1:5–6).

**Illustration**

In the 1940s Henry G. Bosch got a job at Radio Station WMBI, Chicago, operated by Moody Bible Institute. It was wartime and housing was scarce. He and his wife secured temporary quarters in one large backroom but were told they would have to find another place to live shortly. They diligently searched the classified ads as the time drew near for them to move, but to no avail. With only two hours left before they had to vacate their one room, they got down on their knees and asked God to help them find another apartment. So confident was he that God had heard his prayer that he told his wife, as he headed out the door, that he would be back soon with good news. Walking down Dearborn Street, Bosch happened to look up at a nearby building, just as a hand was placing a sign, APARTMENT FOR RENT, in a third-story window. Crossing the street, he told the landlady that she was the answer to their prayers by her action. Although bewildered, she accepted the money for the rent. With joy in his heart, Bosch hurried home to tell his wife the good news, and they spent a joyous ninety minutes carrying their meager belongings to their new home just a block and a half away. They had experienced *the wonders of believing prayer!*[5]

### B. A Thankfulness to God

". . . in everything by prayer and supplication, with thanksgiving, let your requests be made known to God" (4:6). To be thankful in our prayers is to be trustful in our prayers. When we write to a friend in the confidence that he is going to accede to our request, we thank him in advance for what he is going to do. In a similar way, we must realize that answers to our prayers are already formulated in heaven. Ours is not so much to ask for what we need as to claim what is already prepared for us by a loving Father. When we develop this attitude of heart and mind we cannot but celebrate the life of praise.

#### Illustration

Stephen Olford remembers a girl who was on the point of committing suicide. Anxiety had so strangled her will to live that she was a miserable sight to behold. Dr. Olford told her to read through the Book of Psalms and to notice that much of the language is given over to thanksgiving and praise. Several days later she came back to see him, and her face was radiant! She said, "I now set aside one day in the week when I do nothing but thank God, and already I feel well again."

## Conclusion

There is an answer to anxiety. It lies in the mastery of a life of prayer, the therapy of a life of peace, and the victory of a life of praise; and all this is possible through Christ our Lord. To know him is to turn prayer, peace, and praise into "reality therapy." Right now this wonderful Savior waits to enter your life and banish anxiety with his own glorious answer.

# 2

# The Answer to Self-Esteem

## Mark 12:30–31

". . . you shall love [the LORD your God] with all your heart,
. . . soul, . . . mind, and . . . strength. . . . You shall love
your neighbor as yourself . . ." (12:30–31).

## Introduction

There is an aspect of human nature which deserves
nothing less than condemnation and crucifixion. The apostle Paul knew something of this when he cried, ". . . in my
flesh nothing good dwells. . . . O wretched man that I am!
Who will deliver me from this body of death?" (Rom. 7:18,
24). Thank God, provision has been made in the cross of
Jesus Christ to deal not only with our sin but also with
our self-life. To know the redemptive power of Christ's
death is to be able to say, "I have been crucified with
Christ; it is no longer I who live, but Christ lives in me . . ."
(Gal. 2:20). Indeed, it is the function of the Holy Spirit to
apply the mortifying power of Calvary to our sinful flesh in

order that the Christ-life might be magnified in our redeemed personalities. While the death of Christ terminates our condemned selves, that same death liberates our redeemed selves; for let us remember that in being redeemed we do not lose our personal identity. On the contrary, we discover our true identity in all the fullness of the life God intended for us. So there is a part of us which deserves self-esteem.

No one spoke to this point with more authority than our Lord Jesus Christ. He said, ". . . you shall love the LORD your God with all your heart, with all your soul, with all your mind, and with all your strength. . . . You shall love your neighbor *as yourself*. . ." (12:30–31). What we owe to God in terms of unreserved love we owe in like manner to our neighbors and to *ourselves*. The order is plain: God first, others second, and self last—but we must not forget that self is included, even though this is only implied but not *stated* in our text. Exegetically speaking, there are only two commandments that Jesus gave, not three! Assuming that we have discharged our duty to God and our neighbor, we must see to it that we fulfill what Christ taught as the Christian view of self-esteem. Four simple, but important, principles must be observed:

## I. Self-Esteem Demands the Reality of Love

Love yourself with all your heart. Nothing is more detrimental to our human personalities than a heartless love. Such heartlessness may take extreme forms. There is, for instance, the extreme of *stoicism*. Stoicism is indifference to pleasure or pain and produces a callous and calculated character that curses both personal and social life. E. C. McKenzie once said, "The loneliest place in the world is the human heart when love is absent."

**Illustration**

Archbishop Ussher was once wrecked on the coast of Ireland, and almost destitute of clothing he wandered to the house of a clergyman. The ecclesiastic was quite wary and somewhat cold and incredulous. "How many commandments are there?" he suddenly asked, thinking to detect an imposter. "I can at once satisfy you that I am not the ignorant imposter you take me to be," replied the archbishop; "there are eleven commandments." "No," was the sneering comment, "there are but ten commandments in my Bible. Tell me the eleventh and I will give you all the help you need." "There it is," said the archbishop, pointing to this verse: "A new commandment I give unto you, that ye love one another as I have loved you."

The other extreme is that of *sensualism*. There is no heart in that which is sensual or sensuous. It is nothing less than a destructive indulgence which rots the personality and utterly ruins one's testimony to others.

**Illustration**

Some years ago some 7,000 psychologists jammed into Cincinnati for their annual convention. A famed researcher from the University of Illinois, O. Hobart Mowrer, got up and declared: "We psychologists have largely followed the Freudian doctrine that human beings are too good." The patient "has within him impulses, especially those of lust and hostility which he has been unnecessarily inhibiting. And health, we tell him, lies in recognizing and expressing these impulses. . . . As a result, we have largely abandoned belief in right and wrong, virtue and sin."[1]

Self-esteem demands the reality of love, and love only can be real when it is cleansed and controlled by the incoming, indwelling, and infilling of the Holy Spirit. This miracle takes place when we come to God in repentance, and then repose our faith in Jesus Christ as Savior and Lord.

## II. Self-Esteem Demands the Intensity of Love

Love yourself with all your soul. Human love, at best, is sporadic and intermittent. It waxes and wanes because it is determined by the feelings and frustrations of our sinful hearts. This, in turn, adversely affects the human personality. There is only one kind of love which maintains an intensity and that is the love of God. It never fluctuates or vacillates; God's love is faithful and constant, whatever the circumstances.

### Illustration

Mark Guy Pearse used to tell of the time he overheard one of his children admonishing the other, "You must be good or Father won't love you." Calling the boy to him he said, "Son, that isn't really true." "But you won't love us if we are bad, will you?" the boy asked. "Yes, I will love you whether you are good or bad," Pearse explained. "But there will be a difference in my love. When you are good I will love you with a love that makes me glad; and when you are not good I will love you with a love that hurts me."[2]

## III. Self-Esteem Demands the Sagacity of Love

Love yourself with all your mind. A sagacious person is one who is characterized by sound judgment; and this is precisely what it means to love ourselves with all our minds. Paul speaks to this point when he says that no man should ". . . think of himself more highly than he ought to think, but [rather] to think soberly, as God has dealt to each one a measure of faith" (Rom. 12:3).

Once again, there are two extremes that must be avoided in this matter of self-evaluation. The first is that of overestimating ourselves. We are not to think of ourselves more highly than we ought to think because this inevitably leads to our downfall. ". . . God resists the proud, But gives grace to the humble" (James 4:6).

## Illustration

We are all familiar with the ancient fable of the bullfrog who had a conversation with two swans who visited his pond. The frog proudly told the birds of the beauties and sceneries of his underwater home and invited them to join him in an exploration of his territory. The swans gladly obliged. And then it was their turn to describe to him the countryside with its mountains, dales, and pretty hamlets. But the problem arose as to how the frog could travel through the air. Between them they devised a wonderful scheme. The swans agreed to balance a stick between their bills, while the frog held on with his mouth. Then, taking to the air, they showed their bullfrog friend what a wonderful world there was above that muddy pond. For some time they flew over the landscape until they passed a little town where the swans swooped down to give the frog a better view. As they hovered over a group of people, somebody looked up and remarked, "How clever! I wonder who thought of that?" Without hesitation, the frog croaked, "I did," and instantly dropped to the ground. How true is the saying, "Pride goeth before a fall."

The second extreme is just as serious: it is that of underestimating ourselves. Those who are guilty of this are usually introverts who neither honor God, encourage themselves, or bless others. Self-depreciation is often mistaken for humility, but it is nothing of the kind. It is rather an inverted form of pride.

So he who overestimates himself will try to do what he cannot, while he who underestimates himself will not try to do what he can—and in both cases the work is not done. These are two extremes we must avoid. Instead of overestimation or underestimation, there must be the proper estimation of ourselves. This is what Paul means by thinking soberly (see Rom. 12:3). It is accepting what we are in Christ and allowing him to use our capacities for his highest glory.

**Illustration**

Arturo Toscanini conducted Beethoven's Ninth Symphony one evening, giving a brilliant performance. The audience went wild! They clapped, whistled, and stamped their feet with enthusiasm. As Toscanini stood there he bowed repeatedly, then acknowledged his orchestra. When the ovation began to subside, Toscanini turned and looked intently at his musicians. He was almost out of control as he whispered, "Gentlemen! Gentlemen!" The orchestra leaned forward to listen. Was he angry? They could not tell. In a fiercely enunciated whisper, Toscanini said, "Gentlemen, I am nothing." That was an extraordinary admission, since Toscanini was blessed with an enormous ego. He added, "Gentlemen, you are nothing." They had heard that same message before in rehearsal. "But Beethoven," said Toscanini in a tone of adoration, "is everything, everything, everything!" This is the attitude we need toward ourselves and toward the Lord Jesus Christ. I am nothing, you are nothing, he is everything. That was John's attitude. It is the attitude of an authentic messenger of Christ.

It is a tremendous moment when we discover that God does not make duplicates; he only makes originals, and, therefore, there is something which he can say, do, and be in us which cannot be performed in any other life in quite the same way. This true estimation of ourselves comes when we love these redeemed selves soberly and sagaciously.

## IV. Self-Esteem Demands the Activity of Love

Love yourself with all your strength. The sequence is beautiful here. If there is a reality, intensity, and sagacity of love it must issue in an activity of love. God has made us for a purpose, and we shall never be satisfied until that purpose is realized. The Bible tells us that ". . . we are . . . created in Christ Jesus for good works, which God prepared beforehand that we should walk in them" (Eph. 2:10). Our supreme ambition, therefore, should be to find, follow, and finish the plan that God has for our lives. To do so is to know not only fulfillment, but enjoyment. It was said of the Lord Jesus that even when facing the cross he did so ". . . for the joy that was set before Him . . . " (Heb. 12:2). He could also say that his food was ". . . to do the will of Him who sent [him], and to finish His work" (John 4:34). No Christian can live a fulfilled or satisfied life and be a loafer or idler at one and the same time.

### Illustration

According to legend, the angels of heaven, observing the beauty of a noted bishop's life, offered him the power to heal the sick and to perform miracles. The old bishop declined, saying, "The thing I most desire is that God would bestow upon me the gift of doing a great deal of good without even knowing it myself."

Consequently, as the bishop walked upon the earth, wherever his shadow fell the hearts of men cheered, little children laughed, and tired men rested. Humble goodness brings the gift of joy to others.

## Conclusion

We have seen what we mean by the Christian view of self-esteem. It is loving God, loving our neighbor, and then loving ourselves with a reality, intensity, sagacity, and an activity of divine love. The person who lives by these four principles usually has a healthy and happy personality, is a blessing to others, and a pleasure to his God. In these days of psychological abnormalities, how desperately we need sane and balanced people who know the Christian view of self-esteem.

# 3

# The Answer to Care

## *1 Peter 5:6–11*

"Casting all your care upon Him, for He cares for you" (5:7).

## Introduction

Psychiatrists and psychologists are telling us that we live in a fear-ridden age. Never have men and women been so weighed down with corroding care. Indeed, one of the psychological diseases of our time is what is known as "anxiety neurosis." Politicians are worried, businessmen are worried, parents are worried, and even children are worried. Second only to loneliness and boredom, anxiety is the cause of more suicides than anything else we know, and those who do not commit suicide seek escape through alcohol, drugs, or the pursuit of pleasure or business.

The question arises: Is there a cure for care? The Christian answer can be given with a resounding "yes." Peter, in his first epistle, offers these words of comfort, written in an hour of fiery trial and testing: "casting all your care upon Him, for He cares for you" (5:7). As we examine this verse in its immediate context, we discover three simple steps that lead to the cure for care:

## I. We Must Confess to God the Weakness of Our Lives

". . . humble yourselves under the mighty hand of God, that He may exalt you in due time, casting all your care upon Him, for He cares for you" (5:6–7). Man's supreme weakness is his vulnerability to the pride of living independently of God (see Prov. 15:25; 16:18; 1 Tim. 3:6). Indeed, it is this weakness that brought about the first sin in the Garden of Eden. As long as we believe that we can live without the care of God, we are doomed to inevitable anxiety, with all its mental and moral consequences. Therefore, if we would know a cure for care, we must confess the weakness of our lives to God. In other words:

### A. We Must Admit Our Pride Before God

Peter says: ". . . God resists the proud, But gives grace to the humble," and then he adds, ". . . humble yourselves under the mighty hand of God . . ." (5:5–6). This is the hardest thing that you and I have to do, but there is no alternative if we want a life of peace and poise. As long as we maintain a spirit of pride, we are literally fighting against God. In fact, as we have already observed, he sets himself up against pride; he resists the proud, and there is no knowing where such divine resistance will bring us. So we must admit our pride before God.

### B. We Must Accept Our Place Before God

". . . humble yourselves under the mighty hand of God, that He may exalt you in due time" (5:6). There is

only one place from which God exalts a person, and
that is the foot of the cross. The only One who ever had
a right to exalt himself ". . . humbled Himself . . . to the
point of death, even the death of the cross." This is why
"God . . . highly exalted Him and [gave] Him the name
which is above every name, that at the name of Jesus
every knee should bow . . ." (Phil. 2:8–10). Having thus
humbled himself, the Lord Jesus left us an example. The
only difference is that we deserve to be at the foot of
the cross, for we are sinful, wretched, miserable, poor,
and blind. The only language you and I can use is:

> Nothing in my hand I bring,
> Simply to Thy cross I cling.

> Augustus M. Toplady

Therefore, if we would know the cure for care, the
first step is that of confessing our weakness before God.

### Illustration

On one occasion someone said to J. Hudson Taylor,
founder of the China Inland Mission, "You must sometimes
be tempted, Mr. Taylor, to be proud because of the wonderful way God has used you. I doubt if any man living has
had greater honor." To this gracious word Mr. Taylor replied,
"On the contrary, I often think that God must have been
looking for someone small enough and weak enough for
Him to use, and that He found me." In days of stress long
ago the prophet Zechariah declared an undying truth: "Not
by might, nor by power, but by my Spirit, saith the Lord of
Hosts" (Zech. 4:6).[1]

## II. We Must Commit to God the Worries
   of Our Lives

". . . casting all your care upon Him, for He cares for
you" (5:7). It is important to understand the meaning of
that little word "care." It is quite different from God's care,

which we shall consider in a moment. It really means "anxiety" or "worry." In the original, it has the idea of tearing or dividing the heart. Someone has depicted this human care as a little fox terrier pulling a rag doll to pieces. This is what anxiety does to the mind and heart.

But Peter tells us that if we humble ourselves at the foot of the cross, we can commit to God the worries of our lives. He says, "casting all your care upon Him . . ." (5:7). That word "casting" is an energetic word. It is not a question of laying our worries on God, but virtually committing them to God. There are two categories of worry that we are to unload on God:

### A. There Are the Worries About Life

"Casting all your care upon Him . . ." (5:7). In his Sermon on the Mount (see Matt. 6:24–34), our Lord Jesus listed some of the worries that afflict us throughout our lifetime. We worry about food—and we can certainly understand this, in a day when starvation is affecting one-fifth of the world's population; and yet the God who feeds the sparrow has promised to meet the needs of those who will trust him.

We worry about clothes; yet we forget that the God who clothes the grass of the field also provides for his children.

We worry about the future; and yet Jesus said, ". . . do not worry about tomorrow, for tomorrow will worry about its own things. Sufficient for the day is its own trouble" (Matt. 6:34). Only an omniscient God knows what awaits us on the morrow. Albert Einstein once said, "I never think of the future. It comes soon enough."

We could talk about family problems, work problems, health problems, and so on; yet the God who made us is far more concerned than we could ever be about these worries of life.

## B. There Are the Worries About Death

". . . casting all your care upon Him . . ." (5:7). No one in his right mind can escape the fact that ". . . it is appointed for men to die once . . ." (Heb. 9:27). Because of this inevitable appointment with death, we worry about our sin, judgment, and human destiny.

### Illustration

Alfred Krupp, the Prussian [ammunition] manufacturer . . . was so in dread of death himself that it is said that he never forgave anyone who brought up the subject in his presence. All his employees were strictly forbidden, under fear of discharge, to speak of death when he was about. A relative of his wife, who was visiting with them, died suddenly, and Krupp fled from the house in terror. Later, when his wife remonstrated with him about his act, he forsook her and never lived with her again. As he sensed age taking its toll, he offered his physician a sum amounting to one million dollars if he would prolong his life ten years. Of course, the doctor could not guarantee life, and Krupp died.[2]

The amazing thing about it is that even though people do not speak of these matters they sing about them. Analyze modern music today and you will find that there is as much said about evil, death, and judgment as there is about love, sex, and marriage.

What a relief, then, to know that we can commit the worries of our lives to God!

But that is not the whole story. In this passage we have one final thought which we must not overlook:

## III. We Must Commend to God the Watch-Care of Our Lives

"Casting all your care upon Him, for He cares for you" (5:7). The watch-care of God is one of the greatest blessings that the Christian life affords. The word Peter employs here is used elsewhere to describe the activity of a faithful shepherd. This divine activity is realized in our lives through prayer and faith, and is described in this context in three ways:

## A. It Is a Valiant Watch-Care

"He cares for you. Be sober . . ." (5:7–8). When we know the watch-care of God—that divine activity working in us to make us valiant to face life—we don't go to pieces in a crisis; instead, we are self-possessed and controlled. That is the meaning of that little phrase "Be sober" (5:8). So we find ourselves mastering situations instead of being mastered by them.

### Illustration

On March 18, 1979, a twin-engined light plane crashed shortly after takeoff in Aspen, Colorado. Killed were John Edward May, 51, chief executive officer and chairman of the board of May Petroleum; his son, David, 22; his daughter, Karla, 18, and his son-in-law, Richard, 27. For the next two months Mrs. May kept a diary, recording her feelings and emotions. Her entry for May 7 and 8 records: "My burden is heavy, but I don't walk alone. My pain is unrelenting, but I thank God for every moment that He blessed me with. I pray that my life will be used for His glory, that I might carry my burden with Christian dignity, and that out of my devastation . . . His kingdom [may] become apparent to someone lost and in pain. I close this diary, and with it goes all my known ability and capacity for love. I must climb to a different plane and search for a different life. I cannot replace or compare my loss. It is my loss. I am not strong. I am not brave. I am a Christian with a burden to carry and a message to share. I have been severely tested, but my faith has survived, and I have been strengthened in my love and devotion to the Lord. Oh, God, my life is Yours. Comfort me in Your arms and direct my life. I have walked in hell, but now I walk with God in peace. John, David, Karla, and Richard are in God's hands.

I am in God's arms, and His love surrounds me. This rose
will bloom again."

## B. It Is a Vigilant Watch-Care

". . . He cares for you . . . be vigilant . . ." (5:7–8). This
divine watch-care gives us an alertness which sights the
enemy in order that we might fight him. It is a kind of
spiritual radar that makes us aware of the attacks of
Satan. Peter warns that our ". . . adversary the devil
walks about like a roaring lion, seeking whom he may
devour" (5:8). Without the watch-care of God, we are
helpless victims to this powerful adversary. Apart from
God, we are only natural, while Satan is supernatural. It
is very evident that one of the ways in which our enemy
seeks to destroy us is by corroding care.

## C. It Is a Victorious Watch-Care

". . . for He cares for you . . . . Resist him, steadfast
in the faith . . ." (5:8–9). This is the most thrilling
thought of all, for by the power of the God who cares
we can resist the devil at every point of attack and know
day-by-day victory. So Peter tells us that ". . . the God of
all grace, who called us . . . [can] perfect, establish,
strengthen, and settle [us]" in the faith (5:10). This is
how the Lord Jesus Christ lived his life here upon earth,
and he bids us follow him. The thrilling thing is that
he who conquered Satan for us can now conquer Satan
through us.

### Illustration

Martin Luther was asked one time how he overcame the
devil. He replied, "When he comes knocking at the door
of my heart and asks 'Who lives here?' the dear Lord Jesus
goes to the door and says, 'Martin Luther used to live here,
but he has moved out. Now I live here.' The devil, seeing
the nail-prints in His hands, takes flight immediately." Only

the life that has Jesus as a permanent resident can be assured of victory.

## Conclusion

Commit your life to a God who really cares, who has revealed himself through Jesus Christ, and wants to enter that life of yours. Only as we count on him, moment by moment, shall we know the peace of God which passeth all understanding, guarding our hearts and minds in every situation of life.

# 4

# The Answer to Guilt
### *1 John 1:1–7*

"... if we walk in the light as He is in the light, we have fellowship with one another, and the blood of Jesus Christ His Son cleanses us from all sin" (1:7).

## Introduction

Guilt is a fundamental problem of man, and without a remedy he is doomed to abnormal behavior that will ultimately destroy his mental and moral well-being. This is not only the consensus of opinion of those who serve us in the medical profession, but it is the experience of Christian ministers who meet the members of their congregations week by week.

When we turn from the human to the divine aspect of things, we discover that the central message of the Bible concerns this remedy for guilt. This is the reason why God sent his Son into the world to die on Calvary's cross, and this is why there is a gospel to preach.

Perhaps one of the most simple, and yet succinct, statements concerning the remedy for guilt is found in our text. The Bible says, ". . . if we walk in the light as He is in the light, we have fellowship with one another, and the blood of Jesus Christ His Son cleanses us from all sin" (1:7). There are two main things we must notice about the remedy for guilt:

## I. The Divine Provision of this Remedy

". . . the blood of Jesus Christ [God's] Son cleanses . . ." (1:7). Such is the radical problem of guilt that it necessitated the sacrifice of God's only Son in order to provide an adequate remedy. The Bible declares that ". . . without the shedding of blood there is no remission [no forgiveness or cleansing for sin]" (Heb. 9:22). In complete oneness with the Father, Jesus Christ gave his life, even unto death. The shedding of his precious blood means that:

### A. Christ's Death Was Vicarious

". . . the blood of Jesus Christ His Son cleanses us from all sin" (1:7). The word "vicarious" means "representative." Let us remember that Jesus Christ the Son of God was ". . . holy, harmless, undefiled, [and] separate from sinners . . ." (Heb. 7:26). Indeed, it was because he was the spotless One that he could die for men and women who were defiled by guilt.

Paul tells us that the essential message of the gospel is that ". . . Christ died for our sins according to the Scriptures" (1 Cor. 15:3). In some mysterious way that finite minds can never fully understand, Jesus Christ the Son of God bore our sin and our guilt when he died upon the cross. The Bible says that God ". . . made Him who knew no sin to be sin for us, that we might become the righteousness of God in Him" (2 Cor. 5:21). Provision was made for a divine exchange. He took our sinfulness in order that we might take his righteousness. He received our guilt that we might receive his grace. *The Living Bible* states it clearly: ". . . God took the sinless Christ and poured into Him our sins. Then, in exchange, He poured God's goodness into us!" (2 Cor. 5:21). This is the wonder and glory of the Christian gospel.

### Illustration

A wild storm in the north of Scotland threatened the main railway line bridge that spanned a raging stream below. A young shepherd, a Highland laddie, sheltered his sheep as best he could for the night, and in the morning, long before dawn, he set out to see how they fared. As he made his way up the hillside he noticed, to his dismay, that the central column of the viaduct had gone, and the bridge was broken. He knew the mail train was due and, if not warned, would be dashed to pieces and many lives lost. He made his way up as best he could, wondering if he would be in time. As soon as he reached the rails he heard the pound of the mighty engine. He stood and beckoned wildly, but the engineer, making up for lost time, was moving fast. In desperation, the boy flung himself on the tracks, as the engineer applied the brakes. The train came to a screeching halt and the passengers awakened to see what was the matter. After looking around, they recognized the problem and how they had been delivered from a terrible tragedy. A little way along the tracks they saw the mangled remains of the shepherd boy who gave his life for them, dying that they might live.[1]

### B. Christ's Death Was Victorious

". . . the blood of Jesus Christ [God's] Son [goes on cleansing] us from all sin" (1:7). Although the cross was a single event in history, its efficacy is eternal. This is why the present continuous tense is used here—". . . the blood of Jesus Christ [God's] Son [goes on cleansing] us from all sin" (1:7). The life that was released in sacrifice was resurrected in sovereignty. Now, in the power of that endless life, the Lord Jesus Christ goes on cleansing all who have received him by simple faith. This is what Paul means when he says, ". . . it is no longer I who live, but Christ lives in me . . ." (Gal. 2:20); and again: "For to me, to live is Christ . . ." (Phil. 1:21). In every true believer, Jesus Christ the Son of God lives in all his sanctifying grace and glory. As a result, there is constant cleansing—not only from the guilt of sin, but also from the grip of sin. Here, then, is the divine remedy for those who are bound by sin and guilt.

David, the sweet singer of Israel, and later the king of his people, failed miserably when he committed adultery, and then murder. But being a man after God's own heart, he sought the Lord in true penitence and contrition, and he proved the power of the blood of Jesus Christ who, as the Lamb of God, was ". . . slain from the foundation of the world" (Rev. 13:8). So after his experience of cleansing he could exclaim: "Blessed is he whose transgression is forgiven, Whose sin is covered . . ." (Ps. 32:1).

How wonderful to know that ". . . the blood of Jesus Christ [God's] Son cleanses us from ALL sin" (1:7). It matters not what your sin is, God can deal both with its guilt and power.

### Illustration

On the island of Trinidad there is a crater in an extinct volcano which is completely filled with pitch. This asphalt is hard enough for folk to walk on, even though here and there gas escapes in bubbles from its surface. Men dig great chunks from this tar-like lake and load train cars full of it to pave the roads of the world. It is said, however, that no matter how large a hole is made in this Pitch Lake, no cavity will remain after 72 hours, for it immediately fills up from down below. For almost 100 years they have been taking shiploads of asphalt out of this crater, yet it never runs empty. They have gone down as far as 280 feet and still they have found this black, gum-like substance bubbling up. There seems to be an inexhaustible supply. So,

too, with God's grace; it is superabundant, and never dimin-
ishes. No matter how great the need, it cannot exhaust
His love. His grace is sufficient.[2]

## II. The Divine Condition for this Remedy

". . . if we walk in the light as He is in the light, we have
fellowship with one another . . ." (1:7). In these words we
have, in simple terms, what is, in fact, the twofold condition that God lays down for cleansing from guilt:

### A. There Must Be a Truthful Transparency
### in the Presence of God

". . . if we walk in the light as He is in the light . . ."
(1:7). If we want to know the remedy for guilt we have to
be open and honest with God. We must let the light of
his Word and of his Spirit shine into our hearts until
all sin is exposed. Indeed, until we see our sin and guilt
in the searching purity of that light, we may hesitate to
cry to God for mercy. The fact is that in spite of the guilt
that haunts and hurts our lives, we still take pleasure
in sin (see Heb. 11:25b).

### Illustration

The story is told of a midshipman who was put down
into the hold of a vessel as a means of punishment. After
an hour or so, his superior officer went over to the hatch to
find out how the lad was doing. To his surprise—if not to
his disgust—he heard him cheerfully whistling away in the
dark. With set determination to teach this youngster a lesson, the officer lowered a light into the hold of the ship,
and as the filth and vermin became apparent around him,
the midshipman began to plead, "Let me out! Let me out of
this place!" It was the light that made him aware of his
true condition and surroundings. So God's condition is: ". . .
walk in the light as He is in the light . . ." (1:7).

## B. There Must Be a Trustful Dependency on the Person of God

". . . if we walk in the light as he is in the light, we have fellowship with one another . . ." (1:7). In verse 3 of this same passage John tells us: ". . . our fellowship is with the Father and with His Son Jesus Christ." We can only know fellowship with God in Jesus Christ when there is mutual commitment. Christ only commits himself to those who commit themselves to him (see John 2:24–25). When this vertical fellowship is established then we can enjoy a horizontal fellowship with other Christians. And there is nothing in all the world more therapeutic and renewing than Christian fellowship.

Even in medical circles this is being recognized today. This is why there is so much talk and practice of group therapy. Sin isolates and dissipates, whereas salvation integrates and compensates.

This emphasizes the importance of belonging to a local church. People, who once were guilt-ridden to the point of despair, find restoration and fellowship in a caring church. What is true of the church is also true of the home. So God's ultimate aim in redemption is communal fellowship. As John Stott puts it: "The purpose of the proclamation of the gospel is . . . not salvation but *fellowship*. Yet, properly understood, this is the meaning of salvation in its widest embrace, including reconciliation to God in Christ (fellowship . . . with the Father, and with His Son Jesus Christ), holiness of life (see verse 6), and incorporation in the church (you . . . with us)."[3] Thus we need a dependency on God in Christ, and in one another in the spirit of love.

### Illustration

A fish taken out of water gasps for air and quickly perishes. A flower snapped from its stem withers and dies. A Christian removed from the life-sustaining nourishment of the local church begins to fade spiritually and eventually dies. A church home is important not only for teaching, but for fellowship. The church that does not gather into its fold the drunks, the harlots, the liars, and the thieves, does not deserve the right to welcome the saints.

## Conclusion

In the blood of Jesus Christ we find both the provision *of* and the condition *for* the remedy for our guilt. To know this remedy in all its fullness we must be prepared to be open with God and to trust his Son Jesus Christ for complete cleansing. Only then can we sing:

> None other Lamb, None other Name,
> None other hope in heaven or earth or sea;
> None other hiding place from guilt and shame;
> None beside Thee.
>
> Christina Georgina Rossetti

5

# The Answer to Loneliness
## *Psalm 68:5–6*

"A father of the fatherless, a defender of widows is God in His holy habitation. God sets the solitary in families . . ." (68:5–6).

## Introduction

When Janis Joplin was found dead in her hotel room at the age of 27, questions arose as to whether the cause of her death was suicide or an accident. Later the police reported they had found a small quantity of heroin in the rock singer's room. There were also fresh needle marks on her arm. Just before her death she admitted to a friend, "When I am not on the theater stage I just lie around, watch television, and *feel very lonely.*" That one remark, "I . . . feel very lonely," strikes a sympathetic chord in all our hearts, for loneliness is an acute problem that young and old face today.

Thomas Wolfe, an American novelist (1900–1938), once wrote that "loneliness, far from being a rare and curious phenomenon, peculiar to myself and a few other solitary men, is the central and inevitable fact of human existence." The world-famous historian, H. G. Wells, said on his sixty-fifth birthday, "I am sixty-five, and I am lonely." And in more recent times, the late Dag Hammarskjold, former Secretary-General of the United Nations, confessed sadly in his private diary, "Alone beside the moorland spring, once again you are aware of your loneliness as it is and always has been."[1]

As we study the Bible, we discover that God never intended man to be lonely. When he created Adam he saw that it was ". . . not good that man should be alone; [so He made] him a helper comparable to him" (Gen. 2:18). The psalmist tells us that God, who is a father to the fatherless and a protector to the widows, ". . . sets the solitary in families; He brings out those who are bound . . ." (68:5–6). In these words we learn something about the life of loneliness. Observe:

## I. The Misery of Loneliness

"God sets the solitary in families; He brings out those who are bound . . ." (68:6). As we reflect on this condition of loneliness we cannot but be impressed with the accuracy of David's language. Even though his primary reference was to the loneliness of a nation in captivity, the point he makes is true of every lonely life.

### A. There Is the Boredom of Solitude

"God sets the solitary in families . . ." (68:6). The dictionary informs us that solitude is "a state of being solitary, or alone." Such a condition of remoteness from human contact produces all manner of stresses and pressures. Indeed, it is this condition of bored loneliness that often leads to suicide.

### Illustration

A New York City newspaper gave this short story: "The body of a man above seventy years old was recovered from the Spuyten Duyvil Creek yesterday. Police found this note: 'I'm Joe Barnes. No record. No relatives. No friends. No permanent address. Just tired of living.'" It is the sad obituary of a man overcome by the boredom of solitude.[2]

## B. There Is the Bondage of Servitude

"God sets the solitary in families; He brings out those who are bound . . ." (68:6). It is significant to note that in addition to being lonely in Egypt, God's ancient people were also slaves in Egypt.

This is true in our own lives. When we are lonely we sense not only boredom, but bondage. Sometimes it is bondage to people with whom we have no affinity, or else it is bondage to our own fears, failures, and frustrations. Inevitably boredom leads to bondage—and nothing is more miserable! Does that describe your life? Are you lonely and thoroughly miserable?

### Illustration

One New Year's Day a millionaire, whose pride it was never to offer a tip for any service, faced an unforgettable tragedy: his chief accountant committed suicide. The books were found to be in perfect order, the affairs of the dead man—a modest bachelor—were prosperous and calm. The only letter left by the accountant was a brief note to his millionaire employer. It read: "In thirty years I have never had one word of encouragement. I'm fed up!"[3]

## II. The Ministry of Loneliness

"God sets the solitary in families . . . But the rebellious dwell in a dry land, [a desert land]" (68:6). God has so constituted us that when we rebel against him, we end up in a land of desolation and loneliness. In other words:

## A. The Ministry of Loneliness Teaches Us that Rebellion Isolates the Life

". . . the rebellious dwell in a dry [desert] land . . ." (68:6). Perhaps the most telling illustration of this relationship between rebellion and isolation is the story of the Prodigal Son (see Luke 15:11–32). Rebellion not only isolated the son from his father, but also the young man from his so-called "friends." The Bible tells us that he ended up in a field *by himself* feeding pigs. But the redeeming feature is that loneliness brought him to himself, and then back to his father. It is when he came to himself that he said, "I will arise and go to my father . . ." (Luke 15:18). So there is a ministry in loneliness if we are prepared to learn lessons from the disciplines of life.

### Illustration

In one of [Dwight L.] Moody's western campaigns, he was followed from city to city by an aged and broken man of venerable appearance who, in each place, asked the privilege of saying a word to the great congregations. He would stand up and say in a quavering voice, "Is my son George in this place? George, are you here? O George, are you here? O George, if you are here, come to me. Your old father loves you, George, and can't die content without seeing you again." Then the old man would sit down.

One night a young man came to Mr. Moody's hotel and asked to see him. It was George. When the great evangelist asked him how he could find it in his heart to treat a loving father with such cruel neglect, the young man said: "I never thought of him; but Mr. Moody, I have tried to do all the good I could." That is a good picture of a self-righteous prodigal in the far country. He was generous with his money and with his words—yet in every moment of his infamous life he was trampling on the heart of a loving father.[4]

## B. The Ministry of Loneliness Teaches Us that Rebellion Decimates the Life

". . . the rebellious dwell in a dry [desert] land" (68:6). When the prodigal son left home he had pots of money, and plenty of plans, but rebellion led to riotous living, and then to abject poverty. The narrowest letter in the alphabet is the letter "I" and it serves to symbolize how loneliness and sin strip us down to nothingness so that we ". . . dwell in a [desert] land" (68:6).

### Illustration

When Leonardo da Vinci was painting his masterpiece, "The Last Supper," he sought long for a model for his Christ. At last he located a chorister in one of the churches of Rome who was lovely in life and features, a young man named Pietro Bandinelli. Years passed, and the painting was still unfinished. All the disciples had been portrayed save one—Judas Iscariot. Now he started to look for a man whose face was hardened and distorted by sin—and at last he found a beggar on the streets of Rome with a face so villainous he shuddered when he looked at him. He hired the man to sit for him as he painted the face of Judas on his canvas. When he was about to dismiss the man, he said, "I have not yet found out your name." "I am Pietro Bandinelli," he replied. "I also sat for you as your model of Christ." The sinful life of years so disfigured the once fair face of the young man that it now looked as though it were the most villainous face in all Rome! Sin degrades! Sin debases! Sin decimates![5]

This is where God is prepared to meet us, for the Bible reminds us that "Blessed are the poor in spirit, for theirs is the kingdom of heaven" (Matt. 5:3). When a person has truly learned how sin reduces to sinfulness and nothingness it leads him to pray with the hymnist:

> Just as I am, without one plea,
> But that Thy blood was shed for me,

And that Thou bidd'st me come to Thee,
O Lamb of God, I come! I come!

Charlotte Elliott

# III. The Mastery of Loneliness

"God sets the solitary in families; He brings out those who are bound . . ." (68:6). There is an answer to loneliness. As we have stated already, God never intended man to be a lonely and isolated individual. Man is basically social, and therefore must relate to somebody. So we see that:

## A. God Cares for the Lonely

David says, "A father of the fatherless, a defender of widows, is God in His holy habitation. God sets the solitary in families . . ." (68:5–6).

Even though you may feel nobody cares, I want to assure you that God does. He cares for you infinitely. Indeed, he demonstrated this fact by leaving heaven and assuming a human body in order that he might dwell with men and women. Not only did he come to earth, but he died upon a cross in order to make possible the reconciliation of rebellious sinners to a holy and just God. Having died, he rose from the dead to become the Savior and lover of souls. To prove his willingness to share your life, he says, "Behold, I stand at the door and knock. If anyone hears My voice and opens the door, I will come in to him and dine with him, and he with Me" (Rev. 3:20). So the master of loneliness is a God who cares for the lonely.

### Illustration

A man took a tour of a large sheep ranch in Australia at shearing time. During the visit his guide took a baby lamb from its pen and placed it with thousands of other sheep. The noise of their bleating and the shouting of the shearers was deafening. The unweaned animal, looking dazed, remained still for a moment. Then, because it had been separated from its familiar surroundings, it began to let out weak, distressed baa's. Apparently those faint cries were answered immediately by the mother, for the feeble little creature began to walk slowly toward the far end of the enclosure where an old ewe had been standing. The lamb's mother began moving too, rushing to meet that little one as if no other sheep were present. Despite the noise and confusion, she had heard the pitiful bleating of her own frightened offspring. Referring to this incident in a sermon, a minister said, "Don't imagine that you, the object of God's special care, are ever beyond the reach of His attention. The heavenly Father sees you as if there were no other child of His in the whole world. He bends His loving ear to your faintest call for help, and hurries to your aid."[6]

## B. God Calls for the Lonely

"God sets the solitary in families; He brings out those who are bound . . ." (68:6). Ever since Adam rebelled in the Garden of Eden and entered into a state of lonely isolationism, God has been calling out, ". . . Adam, . . . Where are you?" (Gen. 3:9). Adam is but a picture of your life and mine. He is calling us out of our boredom and bondage into his fellowship and freedom. To respond to his call is to know absolute deliverance from loneliness. It does not matter what happens, you can never be alone if you know the God who cares for you and calls for you.

### Illustration

Many years ago a poor German immigrant sat with her children in the waiting room of an Eastern railroad station. A passerby, struck by her look of misery, stopped a moment to speak to her. She confided that her husband had been buried at sea; she was going to Iowa, and it was hard to enter a strange land alone with her babies. The stranger had but one moment. Pressing a little money into the poor creature's hand, she said: "Alone! Why, Jesus is with you! He will never leave you alone!" Ten years afterward the woman said: "That word gave me courage for all my life. When I was a child I knew Christ, and loved Him. I had forgotten Him. That chance word brought me back to Him. It kept me strong and happy through all troubles." That "chance word" was the call of God.[7]

## Conclusion

We have seen something of the misery and ministry of loneliness; but, thank God, there is the mastery of loneliness as well. God gives, and God calls, if only we will respond.

# 6

# The Answer to Hopelessness
## 1 Peter 3:13–16

"But sanctify the Lord God in your hearts, and always be ready to give a defense to everyone who asks you a reason for the hope that is in you, with meekness and fear" (3:15).

## Introduction

We live in a changing world marked by emerging nationalism, terrorism, population explosion, scientific breakthroughs, Star Wars, and the threat of nuclear extinction. But praise God, whatever the changes may be in this or any other age, there are immutables that are ever the same: our Master is the same, our message is the same, and our mission is ever the same. What is urgently needed today is an anointing of the Holy Spirit to relate our unchanging gospel to the changing times.

When Peter wrote his first epistle he was addressing believers who lived in a changing world and were facing the imminent possibility of having to ". . . suffer for right-

eousness' sake . . ." (3:14). In the light of this he urged
them, in verse 15, to have a Christian answer ready.

The day may well come when we, too, shall encounter
persecution for the sake of the gospel. The cold war of
clashing ideologies cannot continue without creating tensions that are bound to snap. When that day arrives we
will have to take a stand and give a Christian witness in
the presence of bitter hatred and vicious opposition. Jesus
promised that the time would come when ". . . whoever
kills you will think that he offers God service" (John 16:2;
see also Matt. 5:11–12). It calls for:

## I. A Christ-Centered Dedication

"But sanctify the Lord God in your hearts . . ."; or to
quote it more accurately from the New American Standard
Bible: "but sanctify Christ as Lord in your hearts . . ." (3:15).
These words imply two very important considerations:

### A. A Recognition of the Saving Christ as Lord

". . . sanctify Christ as Lord . . ." (3:15 NASB). The apostle Paul reminds us that ". . . no one can say that Jesus is
Lord except by the Holy Spirit" (1 Cor. 12:3). The impli-
cation is clear. To name Jesus as Lord is a saving act; it is
where we must begin.

Paul began his Christian experience when he cried,
". . . Lord, what do You want me to do? . . ." (Acts 9:6).
Ever after he made this the basis of his theology. For
him, the recognition of the lordship of Christ not only
indicated the commencement of the Christian life, but
also the climax of the Christian life. He looked forward
to that day when ". . . at the name of Jesus every knee
[will] bow, of those in heaven, and of those on earth,
and of those under the earth, and . . . every tongue [will]
confess that Jesus Christ is Lord, to the glory of God the
Father" (Phil. 2:10–11; see also Rom. 10:9–10).

**Illustration**

Charles Haddon Spurgeon ranks among the greatest preachers of all time. On one particular Sunday evening in London, this nineteenth century Baptist movingly poured out his very soul and life in homage and adoration before his blessed Savior. At the very end, exhausted in body, his voice almost gone, he spoke these words, "Let my name perish, but let Christ's name last for ever! Jesus! Jesus! Crown Him Lord of all! You will not hear me say anything else. These are my last words in Exeter Hall for this time. Jesus! Jesus! Crown *Him* Lord of all!" Knowing Jesus Christ as saving Lord is the first step in a Christ-centered dedication.

### B. A Resignation to the Sanctifying Christ as Lord

". . . sanctify Christ as Lord in your hearts . . ." (3:15 NASB). When we glorify Christ we recognize his perfections. When we magnify him we recognize his greatness. When we justify him we recognize his justice; but when we sanctify him we recognize his holiness; in other words, we hallow Christ as the Lord of holiness in our lives. Peter is teaching here the reality and purity of the indwelling Christ—an indwelling which is to be regarded not only as a subjective experience but also as a subjective expression. Because he indwells our lives we must reverence his presence and power until we reflect that holiness.

To quote Dr. Alexander Maclaren in this regard, we must "take care that our thoughts about Jesus Christ are full of devout awe and reverence. I venture to think that a great deal of modern and sentimental Christianity is very defective in this respect. You cannot love Jesus Christ too much, but you can love Him with too little reverence. And if you take up some of our luscious modern hymns that people are so fond of singing, I think you will find in them a twang of unwholesomeness, just because the love is not reverent enough, and the approaching confidence has not enough of devout awe in it. This generation looks at the half of Christ. When people are suffering from indigestion, they can only see half of the thing they look at, and there are many of us who can only see a part of the whole Christ: and so, forgetting that He is judge, and forgetting that He is the Lion of the tribe of Judah, and forgetting that [while] He is manifested in the flesh [as] our brother He is also God . . . our Creator as well as our Redeemer, and our Judge as well as our Saviour, some do not enough hallow Him in their hearts as Lord."[1]

To sum up our thinking on this point, only as we have high conceptions of the holy Christ who indwells us shall we seek to live out the standard of holiness that he demands and deserves. Is he Lord of your life?

> Lord of every thought and action,
> Lord to send and Lord to stay;
> Lord in speaking, writing, giving,
> Lord in all things to obey;
> Lord of all there is of me,
> Now and evermore to be.
>
> E. H. Swinstead

## II. A Christ-Centered Education

". . . be ready to give a defense to everyone . . ." (3:15). Dedication to Christ prepares us for education, but does not educate us; we must apply our hearts and minds to wisdom under the lordship of Christ. Our text instructs us that this involves:

### A. Academic Teaching

". . . give a defense [or apology] . . ." (3:15). Originally, this was a speech made by a prisoner in his defense, but later the word came to be associated with treatises written in defense of the Christian faith. Doubtless, it is borrowed from the famous *Apologia Socratis.* Such a defense of the faith demands academic training.

It might be argued that Peter was an unlettered man; but remember that his academic teaching was under the greatest tutor the world has ever known, and that for three and a half years. Patristic, scholastic, reformed, and modern theological thought may bore you at times, but under the lordship of Christ it can become an unanswerable argument for the faith you possess.

## B. Systematic Training

". . . be ready to give a defense . . ." (3:15). Readiness to give, to speak, to witness is not the result of teaching alone, but training also. Teaching without training produces proud, cold, and dead intellectualism. An institute of learning must be married to a school of obedience. Training is the implementation of academic teaching under expert direction.

### Illustration

The most valuable training Stephen Olford ever received was in a place known as the Missionary Training Colony on the outskirts of London, England. The purpose and program of this institution was to implement all academic teaching in terms of practical obedience. It involved a daily schedule of life and training that would test every area of Christian character and conduct. At every point of failure there had to be a close examination of the cause of breakdown and the way of victory. Looking back at the experience, Stephen Olford says that he learned more of God and his ways in his two years at the Colony than in any other similar period of his life.

## III. A Christ-Centered Presentation

". . . be ready to give a defense to everyone who asks you a *reason* for the hope that is in you, with meekness and fear" (3:15). If there is a Christ-centered dedication and education, you can expect a Christ-centered presentation which is:

## A. Reasonable

". . . be ready to give a . . . reason . . ." (3:15). The word translated "reason" is *logos,* implying a thoughtful and reasoned explanation. So much of preaching and witnessing today is just unrelated scriptural texts and evangelical cliches. God forgive us! To reflect the divine mind is to ". . . bring every thought to the obedience of Christ" (2 Cor. 10:5).

## B. Reliable

". . . the hope that is in you . . ." (3:15). The message of the Bible is one of hope. Summing up the teaching of the Old Testament, Paul says: "For whatever things were written before were written for our learning, that we through the patience and comfort of the Scriptures might have hope" (Rom. 15:4). The patriarchs looked on in hope, the poets sang in hope, and the prophets declared their flaming messages in hope of the coming Messiah. Then he came, lived, died, rose again, and ascended on high to return one day to consummate all the hopes of the past, present, and future.

The New Testament message is one of hope. To quote the apostle Paul again: "Therefore, having been justified by faith, we have peace with God through our Lord Jesus Christ, through whom also we have access by faith into this grace in which we stand, and rejoice in hope of the glory of God" (Rom. 5:1–2). What a message of radiance and relevance to a world that is lost and hopeless! Ours is a message of hope and we must not forget it.

### Illustration

When two Iraqi missiles smashed into the *USS Stark* in the Persian Gulf in May of 1987, 35 American seamen were killed. Before the bodies were loaded aboard a U.S. military jet to be shipped back to the States, there was a solemn airport ceremony attended only by Mrs. Barbara Kiser, wife of one of the victims, and her five-year-old son. "I don't have to mourn or wear black," she said, "because I know my husband is in heaven. He's better off. God doesn't make mistakes." What a testimony of hope! Here was a woman who could speak from personal experience of her hope in the Lord.

No man has a reliable testimony until he says that he has *a living hope*—"Blessed be the God and Father of our Lord Jesus Christ, who according to His abundant mercy has begotten us again to a living hope through the resurrection of Jesus Christ from the dead" (1 Peter 1:3); *an indwelling hope*—". . . Christ in you, the hope of glory" (Col. 1:27); *an assuring hope*—"This hope we have as an anchor of the soul, both sure and steadfast . . ." (Heb. 6:19); *a purifying hope*—"And everyone who has this hope in Him purifies himself, just as He is pure" (1 John 3:3). Unless the radiance and reality of a personal experience of Christ accompanies our presentation, all the education in the world will amount to nothing.

### Illustration

A Hindu convert in India could neither read nor write, but he got others to read the Bible to him. His favorite verse was John 1:12—"As many as received Him, to them gave He the power to become the sons of God." "I have received Him," said he, "so I have become a son of God." He went back to his village radiantly happy. "I have become a son of God," he cried. His life was so transformed, and his simple witness so effective, that the villagers all wanted to become "sons of God," too.[2]

### C. Respectable

". . . with meekness and fear" (3:15); that is, not with arrogance and self-assertion, but with due respect toward men and reverence before God. With some hearers, the spirit in which a statement is made may matter more than its contents. Only if they are attracted by the former will they give a proper hearing to the latter.

Then adds the apostle Peter: "having a good conscience, that when they defame you as evildoers, those who revile your good conduct in Christ may be ashamed" (3:16). The acid test of a worthy presentation of Christ is a good conscience toward God and a good commendation before men.

## Conclusion

We have seen what constitutes the Christian answer: a Christ-centered dedication, education, and presentation. Have you prepared yourself for the one and only answer you can give to our generation, in this hour of confusion, frustration, and tension? If you have, then dedicate yourself to Christ as Lord, and then use your Christian education and presentation to win a lost world for Christ and his kingdom.

# 7

# The Answer to Suffering
## 2 Corinthians 12:7–10

"My grace is sufficient for you, for My strength is made perfect in weakness . . ." (12:9).

## Introduction

Suffering is a fact of life. To attempt to dispute it or dismiss it is utterly foolish, for it is all around us. We see it in the home, etched in the face of an ailing loved one. We hear it from the streets in the agonizing groans of some victim mugged by thugs. We catch it in the news from war-torn areas of the world.

Suffering has been the lot of all people, including the greatest men of God who ever lived. Of these we could mention such biblical characters as Job, Jeremiah, Paul, and of course, our Lord himself. George MacDonald says that "the Son of God suffered unto death, not that men might not suffer, but that their sufferings might be like His."

As we consider the subject of suffering, think particularly of Paul the apostle. Throughout his life he experienced what he termed ". . . a thorn in the flesh . . ." (12:7). Martin Luther maintained that this affliction represented the opposition and persecution which Paul had to face. John Calvin's view was that the thorn symbolized spiritual temptation. Our Roman Catholic friends stoutly held that the thorn suggested a sexual problem. Then there are others who argue from the Scriptures (Gal. 4:15; 6:11) that in all probability the thorn in the flesh was a form of eye trouble, stemming from the blinding glory that Paul experienced on the Damascus road (see Acts 9:9). Still others speculate that his problem was malaria, epilepsy, insomnia, and particularly depression. The truth is we just don't know. This may be providential and consequential, because his experience helps us to understand our own sufferings and how to rise above them.

There is an answer to suffering, and this is clearly brought out in the text before us. Consider, first of all:

## I. There Is a Mystery in Suffering

Paul says, ". . . lest I should be exalted above measure by the abundance of the revelations, a thorn in the flesh was given to me, a messenger of Satan to buffet me . . ." (12:7). We cannot read these words in the context of the Bible without coming to the conclusion that the problem of suffering is enveloped in mystery. There are, however, two facts that we need to bear in mind as we attempt to unravel the mystery:

### A. The Mystery in Suffering Is Linked with the Morality of God's Creatures

Paul says, ". . . a thorn in the flesh was given to me . . ." (12:7). Strange as it may seem, his suffering is traced to the permissive action of an all-wise God. When

God created angels, and later man, he did not produce robots; on the contrary, he brought into being personalities capable of moral decisions. To have done anything less would have failed to express his own character. In view of this, man is free to choose to enthrone God or to dethrone him. The Bible teaches that Satan chose to dethrone God. Adam did likewise in the Garden of Eden and, through this moral sin of rebellion, suffering inevitably followed. Suffering, therefore, has become part of human life; something to be accepted until that day when God will remove all sin from this world and usher in ". . . new heavens and a new earth in which righteousness dwells [forever]" (2 Peter 3:13).

### Illustration

Herbert Lockyer has a book entitled "Dark Threads the Weaver Needs." It's a book on human suffering and how we wrestle with it. Mr. Lockyer titled his book after a poem written by an unknown Christian author. That poem reads like this:

My life is but a weaving, between my Lord and me;
I cannot choose the colours, He worketh steadily.
Ofttimes He weaveth sorrow and I, in foolish pride,
Forget He sees the upper and I the underside.
Not till the loom is silent and the shuttles cease to
fly,
Shall God unroll the canvas and explain the reason
why
The dark threads are as needful in the Weaver's
skillful hand,
As the threads of gold and silver, in the pattern He
has planned.

## B. The Mystery in Suffering Is Linked with the Mortality of God's Creatures

". . . a thorn in the flesh was given to me . . ." (12:7), says Paul. In this very statement he spells out his own mortality. When Adam sinned he affected himself and the whole of the human race, for the Bible says, ". . . through one man sin entered the world, and death through sin . . ." (Rom. 5:12). Because man is mortal he is subject to all manner of infirmities. It is true that temperament, environment, bereavement, or ailment may accentuate the various forms of suffering; but the fact remains that suffering is a problem to be reckoned with. Sometimes it may mean spiritual suffering; other times, mental suffering; but, most frequently, physical suffering.

### Illustration

Georgi Vins spent most of 15 years in prison—three at hard labor. He was completing his third five-year sentence to be followed by five years of exile in Siberia. Suddenly he was given a suit, a shirt, a tie and told that he was being stripped of Soviet citizenship. Within 48 hours he found himself in the United States. His mother at 68 was arrested and sentenced to three years in prison for aiding Christians. He was only seven the last time he saw his father, who died in prison. When Bill Moyers interviewed Vins he said, "Your father died in prison, your mother was arrested. You've spent much of your life in prison. You once wrote, 'Our life has not been given for empty dreaming,' what has it all meant? What do you think your lives signify?" His reply: "I do not regret the years I have spent, even the years of suffering. This has been the purpose of my living."

## II. There Is an Agony in Suffering

". . . a thorn in the flesh was given to me . . ." (12:7). When Paul speaks of his "thorn in the flesh," he uses a word which does not appear on the surface. The term "thorn" means a "stake," and it seems as if Paul elected to use this word in order to convey the intensity of suffering which he experienced throughout his life.

## A. The Extent of this Suffering

". . . a thorn in the flesh was given to me, a messenger of Satan to buffet me . . ." (12:7). In the sovereignty of God, this "messenger of Satan" was allowed to assault and attack the apostle at every corner of the road. The word "buffet" means "to strike with the blow of the fist," and so conveys the idea of shame and humiliation. As we study the life of the apostle, it seems that he was ever up against the devil. In Cyprus he had to face Elymas the sorcerer, who Paul described as the ". . . son of the devil . . ." (Acts 13:10). In Thessalonica the devil prevented him from visiting that church (see 1 Thess. 2:18). In Ephesus he tells us that he "fought with beasts" (1 Cor. 15:32); and later, writing to that same church, he declares, " . . . we do not wrestle against flesh and blood, but against principalities, against powers, against the rulers of the darkness of this age, against spiritual hosts of wickedness in the heavenly places" (Eph. 6:12).

## B. The Effect of this Suffering

"Concerning this thing I pleaded with the Lord three times that it might depart from me. And He said to me, 'My grace is sufficient for you . . .'" (12:8-9). As long as we are in this world we shall suffer pain. That God allows this has already been established. But the devil also employs the thorn. What determines triumph or defeat, however, is finally decided by the effect of the pain. If it leads to resistance and resentment, then the consequence is one of depression and despair. On the other hand, if the pain leads to prayerfulness and patience, then the result is one of maturity and victory. Like his Master before him, Paul prayed three times for deliverance from the thorn in the flesh. He asked for faith and persistence, but the thorn was never removed.

Instead, the answer from heaven was, ". . . My grace is
sufficient for you, for My strength is made perfect in
weakness . . ." (12:9).

## III. There Is a Victory in Suffering

". . . most gladly I will rather boast in my infirmities,
that the power of Christ may rest upon me. Therefore I
take pleasure in infirmities, in reproaches, in needs, in
persecutions, in distresses, for Christ's sake. For when I
am weak, then I am strong" (12:9–10). Paul here reaches
the climax of his subject. Suffering certainly means
agony, but it can also mean victory. As long as we walk
the pilgrim pathway we shall know joy and we shall
experience sorrow; but the evidence of having learned
the lessons in the school of obedience is that we emerge
". . . more than conquerors through Him who loved us"
(Rom. 8:37). This victory in Christ is determined by the
exercise of our faith.

### A. There Is a Test of Faith

"Therefore I take pleasure in infirmities, in reproaches, in needs, in persecutions, in distresses, for
Christ's sake. For when I am weak, then I am strong"
(12:10). Imagine a man saying, "I take pleasure in infirmities, in reproaches, in necessities, in persecutions, in
distresses, for Christ's sake." This is victory.

#### Illustration

The story is told of a man who was asked to visit a lady
dying of an incurable and painful disease. He took with him
a little book of cheer for those in trouble. "Thank you very
much," she said, "but I know this book." "Have you read it
already?" asked the visitor. With a smile on her face, the
woman replied, "I wrote it."

Faith in our Lord who suffered even unto death is victory in times of affliction and depression. In the place of weakness he ministers his grace and strength.

## B. There Is a Rest of Faith

". . . most gladly I will rather boast in my infirmities, that the power of Christ may rest upon me," or more literally, that "the dynamism of Christ might overshadow me" (12:9). Paul knew that as long as he gloried in his infirmities a tabernacle of power would overshadow him. In his weakness was the secret of his strength. On the other hand, if and when he gloried in anything other than his infirmities, that tent of power would be removed.

Electric power comes from the pressure of accumulated masses of water backed up by a dam and forced through turbines which generate electricity. Steam power comes by fire which heats water until it expands and creates pressure in a cylinder. Gasoline power is the explosion of a volatile liquid in a chamber called a cylinder, thus setting in motion a piston head and crankshaft.

In a similar way, as we rest by faith in Christ to employ what he pleases to discipline our lives, we find that the very pressures he uses are transmitted into power. The moment we resist, the power is removed; as we rest in faith, the power remains. This is what we might term "the strength of suffering." Instead of being a problem, suffering can become a redemptive power.

### Illustration

George Matheson, noted poet and man of God, lost his sight as a youth and spent 30 years in darkness. The third stanza of one of his widely-known songs reads:

O Joy that seekest me through pain,
I cannot close my heart to Thee;

I trace the rainbow through the rain,
And feel the promise is not vain
That morn shall tearless be.

He had learned to live with his darkness. More than that, he had learned to be benefitted by his handicap. His victory is seen in the words he once wrote: "My God, I have never thanked thee for my thorn. I have thanked thee one thousand times for my roses, but never once for my thorn. I have been looking forward to a world where I shall get compensation for my cross, but never thought of my cross as a present glory. Teach me the glory of my cross. Teach me the value of my thorn. Show me that I have climbed to Thee by the path of pain. Show me that my tears have been my rainbow.[1]

## Conclusion

History is replete with illustrations of people who have been used in the world because they have suffered. The supreme example is our Lord Jesus Christ who, through his suffering on the cross, provided us with forgiveness, freedom, and fruitfulness. Let us then kneel at the foot of that cross and bow to the Holy Spirit who enabled him to suffer, even unto death, to produce in us the same fruits of victory. There is mystery in suffering; yes, agony, but, thank God, there is also victory!

# 8

# The Answer to Fearfulness
## 1 John 4:11–18

"There is no fear in love; but perfect love casts out fear . . ."
(4:18).

## Introduction

The problem of fear is as old as the existence of man. From the moment our first parents separated themselves from their Creator through an act of disobedience, man has been haunted by fear.

To obviate any confusion in our minds, however, it might be well to point out that the Bible speaks of two kinds of fear. There is a filial fear which is God-given. It enables man to reverence God's authority, obey his commands, and hate and shun all forms of evil (see Jer. 32:14; Heb. 5:7). Filial fear is the beginning of wisdom (see Ps. 111:10), the secret of happiness (see Prov. 8:13), a feature of the people in whom God delights (see Ps. 147:11), and the whole duty of man (see Eccles. 12:13).

But the Bible also speaks of slavish fear which is a natural consequence of sin and the expectation of judgment. Solomon says, "The wicked flee when no one pursues, But the righteous are bold as a lion" (Prov. 28:1). When Paul ". . . reasoned about righteousness, self-control, and the judgment to come, Felix [the governor] was afraid . . ." (Acts 24:25). And when the earthquake shook the foundations of the prison, Luke tells us that the Philippian jailer ". . . called for a light, ran in, and fell down trembling before Paul and Silas. And he brought them out and said, 'Sirs, what must I do to be saved?'" (Acts 16:29–30). Such a fear as this can paralyze the lives of men and women unless a way of deliverance is found.

The passage before us speaks of:

## I. The Tyranny of Fear

"Fear involves torment" (4:18). Walk the streets of our metropolitan cities and observe the faces that you pass. The furrowed brows, the haggard faces, the staring eyes, and sometimes the trembling hand, are all evidence of the tyranny of fear.

What is the cause of such tyranny? The answer is twofold:

### A. An Ultimate Cause of Fear

Because of ". . . the day of judgment . . . fear involves torment . . ." (4:17–18). Although these words are addressed primarily to Christians, they also have a message to men and women who know nothing of the grace of God, for they, too, are aware of the inevitability of death and the indispensability of divine judgment. The Bible says, ". . . it is appointed for men to die once, but after this the judgment" (Heb. 9:27). Though projects are launched to try to extend the life of mankind by bio-

logical research, yet the fact must be faced that ultimately it is appointed for men to die.

### Illustration

It is an anthropological fact that the fear of death is uni-
versal, whether a person lives in a primitive land or a civi-
lized country. Stephen Olford recalls watching brave A-Chokwe
tribesmen in Africa flinging spears at one another to see
who could take the most punishment before they collapsed
through loss of blood. He also spoke to these same men
and learned that, deep down in their hearts, they were
afraid to die.

One of the greatest proofs that there is a day of judgment coming is that men and women the world over
are agreed on the need of justice. Indeed, our very sense
of justice—however warped and weak—is a projection
of the Creator's handiwork in our lives. Let us remember
that God is the Judge of all the earth (see Gen. 18:25);
therefore, every human being will one day have to stand
before the judgment throne of God to give an account
of every word and action. This is why "fear involves
torment" (4:18). The very thought of death and coming
judgment creates fear in the hearts of those who have
no confidence to stand in the day of judgment.

### B. An Immediate Cause of Fear

"Fear involves torment" (4:18). The Bible makes it
clear that there are three main reasons why men and
women fear death and judgment. These constitute the
immediate cause of fear. Let us examine these reasons
for a moment:

#### 1. A SENSE OF GUILT

When Adam and Eve tried to hide themselves from
the presence of the Lord among the trees of the Garden of Eden, he confessed, ". . . I was afraid because I

was naked; and I hid myself" (Gen. 3:10). However we may try to rationalize human sin, we are still plagued by guilt. Even the most hardened criminals will admit to a sense of guilt. The word *guilt* and its derivatives occur some thirty times in the Bible. In the New Testament, it means to be under judgment (see Rom. 3:19) and worthy of punishment (see 1 Cor. 11:27; James 2:10). As someone has put it, "No great progress need be traced in the development of the concept of guilt. Cain was as guilty as David"—and we could add, you are as guilty as I am.

**Illustration**

Some years ago a woman serving a life prison term confessed to three additional slayings in which she was involved ten years earlier, which had never been reported. It was only after she was incarcerated that the memory of her crimes began to affect her conscience. The "weights" of guilt were too much for her to bear and began to work on her. Even though she realized that she might spend additional time in prison or be sentenced to death she had to declare the wrong she had done in order to try to make amends for killing these people.

**2. A LACK OF PEACE**

Paul says, "Be anxious for nothing, but in everything by prayer and supplication, with thanksgiving, let your requests be made known to God; and the peace of God, which surpasses all understanding, will guard your hearts and minds through Christ Jesus" (Phil. 4:6–7). Where there is no peace there is worry, and where there is worry there is underlying fear. The most sought after titles in literature today are books on peace, serenity, and composure. The reason for this, of course, is obvious: we are living in a fear-ridden age. While this has been true throughout the centuries, it is perhaps more acute today because of the consequences of our scientific advancements. Instead of beating our swords into plowshares, and our spears into pruning hooks (see Isa. 2:4; Micah 4:3), we have manufactured engines of war capable of reducing our planet to a cinder.

### Illustration

Professor Harold Urey, Nobel Prize winner in chemistry at the early age of 41, and whose work prepared the atomic bomb, wrote a pamphlet entitled, "I'm a Frightened Man." As a member of the Uranium Committee on the key operation of U-235, he said: "I write to frighten you. I am a frightened man myself. All the scientists I know are frightened—frightened for their lives—and frightened for your life."[1]

### 3. THE NEED OF CHRIST

The Bible tells us that Christ "is our peace" (see Eph. 2:13–14). One of his favorite expressions, used when addressing individuals and groups here upon earth, was "Fear not" (Matt. 10:28; Luke 5:10; 8:50). He knew that men and women ". . . through fear of death were all their lifetime subject to bondage" (Heb. 2:15), so he came to dispel fear by cleansing their sins and giving them his peace.

Now even though there are a thousand and one subsidiary causes of fear that we could enumerate, basically they all originate from the ultimate cause of fear which is death and judgment; and then the immediate cause, which is a sense of guilt, a lack of peace, and, supremely, the need of Christ.

## II. The Mastery of Fear

"There is no fear in love; but perfect love casts out fear, because fear involves torment. But he who fears has not been made perfect in love" (4:18). Here is one of the greatest statements to be found in the Bible. It tells us that the perfect love which Jesus has revealed and released in Jesus Christ is able to cast out fear and bring us peace. John gives us the secret of this mastery of fear in the verses before us:

## A. There Must Be the Confession of the Son of God

"Whoever confesses that Jesus is the Son of God, God abides in him, and he in God" (4:15). Since God is love, and we can never know this love until God reveals himself in Jesus Christ, we must take the first step of confessing the Son of God. We are told that ". . . the Father has sent the Son as Savior of the world" (4:14). Therefore, to confess that Jesus is the Son of God is to accept Christ as our Savior from sin and guilt and fear.

## B. There Must Be the Possession of the Spirit of God

"By this we know that we abide in Him, and He in us, because He has given us of His Spirit" (4:13). The ministry of the Holy Spirit is to make Jesus real in our lives. We can never know the Son of God, nor the wonder of his love, until we have been regenerated by the Spirit of God. When this quickening takes place we become possessed of the fruit of the Spirit which is ". . . love, joy, peace, longsuffering, kindness, goodness, faithfulness, gentleness, self-control . . ." (Gal. 5:22–23).

## C. There Must Be the Expression of the Service of God

". . . If we love one another, God abides in us, and His love has been perfected in us" (4:12). By confessing the Son of God we establish the relationship of love. By possessing the Spirit of God we experience the resourcefulness of love. By expressing the service of God we enjoy the release of love. It is important to observe that nowhere in the Bible are we encouraged to be introspective in our love. Rather, we should express the service of love by seeking men and women who need to know this glorious message which banishes the tyranny of fear. A person who has a living relationship to Jesus Christ and knows the indwelling of the Holy Spirit and is busy in loving others is one who has proved the truth of those words, "There is no fear in love; but perfect love casts out fear . . ." (4:18).

### Illustration

Dr. Watson tells of once hearing a plain sermon in a little country church. It was a layman, a farmer, who preached, but Dr. Watson said he never heard so impressive an ending to any sermon as he heard that day. After a fervent presentation of the Gospel, the preacher said with great earnestness: "My friends, why is it that I go on preaching to you week by week? It is just this, because I can't eat my bread alone." That is the master's burden. He cannot bear to be alone in his joy. There is no surer test of love for Christ than the longing to have others love Him.[2]

## Conclusion

God has promised us ". . . a spirit . . . of power and of love and of a sound mind" (2 Tim. 1:7). Therefore, we do not need to live in the grip of the tyranny of fear, but we can choose to live in the glory of the mastery of fear. Step out of fear into faith by confessing the Son of God, possessing the Spirit of God, and then expressing the service of God in a life of love for others.

# The Answer to Temptation

## 1 Corinthians 10:6–13

"No temptation has overtaken you except such as is common to man; but God is faithful, who will not allow you to be tempted beyond what you are able, but with the temptation will also make the way of escape, that you may be able to bear it" (10:13).

## Introduction

If ever a man lived under pressure it was Paul the apostle. This is evident from a reading of the Acts of the Apostles and some of his epistles. In one characteristic passage he talks about being ". . . hard pressed on every side, yet not crushed; . . . perplexed, but not in despair; persecuted, but not forsaken; struck down, but not destroyed" (2 Cor. 4:8–9). Yet this amazing man always seemed to find a way of escape. When faced with tragedy he invariably came through to victory. Paul, therefore, uniquely qualifies to speak to this subject.

Are you facing temptation? If so, are you surviving or going under? Whatever your experience, you are going to be helped by the words of Paul. To this man, all pressure was a form of temptation or testing; ". . . but God is faithful, who will not allow you to be tempted beyond what you are able, but with the temptation will also make the way of escape, that you may be able to bear it" (10:13). Notice:

## I. The Certainty of Temptation

"No temptation has overtaken you except such as is common to man . . ." (10:13). Paul is quite certain that temptation is a certainty of life, and that for two reasons:

### A. Temptation Is Common to Man

"No temptation has overtaken you except such as is common to man . . ." (10:13). In the immediate context, Paul tells us about five different kinds of temptation which have assailed man since the beginning of history:

#### 1. THERE IS THE TEMPTATION TO LUST

"Now these things became our examples, to the intent that we should not lust after evil things as they also lusted" (10:6). The temptation of lust takes us back to Numbers 22, where the Hebrew people despised the manna which God had provided and lusted for the fish, the cucumbers, the melons, the onions, and the garlic of Egypt (see Num. 11:5); in other words, the things that were outside the divine provision.

Perhaps this is one of the strongest temptations for the Christian. Despite all that God gives us, in terms of his guidance, deliverance, assurance, and sustenance, we look back to the life we once lived and long for it with fleshly desire. The tragedy of this spiritual state is that God often grants our request, but in so doing sends leanness into our souls (see Ps. 106:15). Is there leanness in your soul? If so, you can take it for granted that you have been craving something which is outside the purpose of God for your life. Remember that ". . . when desire has conceived, it gives birth to sin; and sin, when it is full-grown, brings forth death" (James 1:15). God save us from the barrenness of a life of unholy desires!

## 2. THERE IS THE TEMPTATION TO IDOLATRY

". . . do not become idolaters as were some of them. As it is written, 'The people sat down to eat and drink, and rose up to play'" (10:7). This is a reference to Exodus 32 where the people became restless and impatient, because of the long absence of Moses in the holy mount. Aaron, therefore, was asked to fashion a god which they could worship and sacrifice to. It is recorded that Aaron took the golden earrings which the people provided, melted them down in the fire, and with an engraving tool made a molded calf (see Exod. 32:4). Not only did they claim that the golden calf was the god who had brought them out of Egypt, but they indulged in unrestrained singing and dancing (see Exod. 32:18, 19, 25). The reference here is to the festivities and debauchery which were associated with idol worship. In the very act of such worship their lower passions were unleashed.

What a warning this should be to us who live in an age of accentuated idolatry! Think of the many things people have substituted for God: an affluent lifestyle in terms of their homes, clothes, and automobiles; preoccupation with work; the adulation of film and rock stars; and excessive interest in sports, and the pursuit of pleasure. As Christians, we often go through the outward motions of attending church and reading our Bibles, but know little of inward reality. Even our churches are characterized by activity instead of ministry. Says Dr. Warren Wiersbe, "A Sunday bulletin that looks like an airlines timetable does not always indicate that God's people are serving the Lord. It could mean that they are living on substitutes. The mature pastor is not against activity, because he knows that Spirit-filled people will be busy serving others; but he does not make activity the sole test of the spiritual level of the church."[1]

Whenever we depend upon some thing, instead of the eternal Someone, we have fallen to the temptation of idolatry. The moment this happens our religion becomes easy. It is a matter of eating, drinking, dancing, or giving vent to our lower natures and so life's pressures begin to mount. Oh, how the apostle John felt the pressure of this very temptation in his day, when he exhorted, "Little children, keep yourselves from idols . . ." (1 John 5:21). How we need to pray:

> The dearest idol I have known,
> Whate'er that idol be,
> Help me to tear it from Thy throne,
> And worship only Thee.
>
> William Cowper

### 3. THERE IS THE TEMPTATION TO FORNICATION

"Nor let us commit sexual immorality as some of them did, and in one day twenty-three thousand fell" (10:8). Read Numbers 25 carefully and observe how the children of Israel prostituted their liberty in God by courting the daughters of Moab. This was an "unequal yoke" which God had forbidden. Because they disobeyed the law of God judgment came upon the people and 24,000 perished in a day. Note that Paul mentions only 23,000. The obvious explanation is that Paul was making allowance for those slain by the judges (see Num. 25:5). Study the Scriptures carefully on this subject and you will find that whenever the children of Israel sought to marry outside the expressed will of God fornication and even worse sins inevitably followed.

### 4. There Is the Temptation to Unbelief

"Nor let us tempt Christ, as some of them also tempted, and were destroyed by serpents" (10:9). Our illustrative mention here is Numbers 21. The people had become weary of the journey and began to speak against God and Moses. They tempted God in the spirit of unbelief and so were "destroyed by serpents" (10:9).

How easy it is to become weary in well doing and to begin to tempt God by our unbelief! Instead of exercising faith in his ability to work all things for our good and his glory, we hinder his working in our lives and in our churches by calculated unbelief—and God has to judge this. Just as he sent fiery serpents in Moses' day, so he allows Satan to attack us with his deadly poison in our day. Remember, nothing straitens God in the fulfilling of his purposes in our lives more than the sin of unbelief (see Matt. 13:58).

### 5. There Is the Temptation to Murmuring

"Nor murmur, as some of them also murmured, and were destroyed by the destroyer" (10:10). Undoubtedly, Paul had Numbers 14:2 in mind. The occasion was the evil report brought by the ten spies concerning the giants they had seen in Canaan. This led to murmuring and God's displeasure; so he overthrew the children of Israel in the wilderness.

This is a solemn lesson indeed! Perhaps the reason why God forbids so many Christians from entering into the fullness of the blessing of life in Canaan is because of the sin of murmuring. It means "to complain" or "to mutter against," and is undoubtedly the most popular of all the five sins that have been enumerated in this context. God says that the penalty for this sin is exclusion from all that Canaan represents in terms of victory, fruitfulness, and rest in Christ. George Sweeting says: "Contentious tongues have hindered the work of God a thousand times over. Critical tongues have closed church doors. Careless tongues have broken hearts and [the] health of many pastors. The sins of the tongue have besmirched the pure white garments of the Bride of Christ."[2]

### B. Temptation Is Common to Christ

"No temptation has overtaken you except such as is common to man . . ." (10:13). We must remember that Jesus Christ was the Son of man as well as the Son of God. As man, he was severely tempted ". . . in all points . . . as we are, yet without sin" (Heb. 4:15). In the wilderness, Satan tempted him in the area of the spirit, the soul, and the body; yet he triumphed gloriously. He faced temptation in the Garden of Gethsemane: the choice of some easier plan or accepting the "cup" of suffering on Calvary's cross. Strengthened by an angel after agonizing in prayer, he could say to his Father, ". . . not My will, but Yours, be done" (Luke 22:42). Even while hanging on the cross, he was not beyond testing. Reviled by the two thieves and those who passed by, he was urged, if he were the Son of God, to come down from the cross and save himself (see Matt. 27:40–44). If Jesus Christ was tempted like that how can we expect to be excluded from similar testing?

## II. The Character of Temptation

". . . God is faithful, who will not allow you to be tempted beyond what you are able . . ." (10:13). An understanding of these words makes it evident that the character of temptation is designed to do two things:

## A. It Exposes the Feebleness of Man

"Therefore let him who thinks he stands take heed lest he fall" (10:12). The application of these words of warning is clear and challenging. The Christians in Corinth were cocksure of their spiritual state; but so were the Israelites—and they reaped disaster. So will we *if we are self-confident*. In and of ourselves we can never conquer temptation. We are slow to learn this lesson so we are constantly tested in order to expose our feebleness. This is why Paul insists on the need for vigilance (10:12).

### Illustration

Again and again a fortress has been stormed because its defenders thought it could not be. In Revelation 3:3 the risen Christ warns the Church at Sardis to be on the watch. The Acropolis of Sardis was built on a spur of rock that was held to be impregnable. When Cyrus was besieging it, he offered a special reward to anyone who could find a way in. One day a soldier who was watching noticed a member of the Sardian garrison drop his helmet accidentally over the battlements. He saw him climb down the precipice after it and marked his path. That night he led a band up the cliff by that very path, and when they reached the top they found the battlements completely unguarded. Life is a chancy business; we must ever be on the watch.[3]

## B. It Discloses the Faithfulness of God

". . . God is faithful, who will not allow you to be tempted beyond what you are able . . ." (10:13). Because God is omniscient he knows all the circumstances that are associated with the testings and pressures of life. He also knows our feebleness which he complements with his divine strength in order to make us victors, instead of victims, over life's temptations. Here, then, is something on which we can rely completely—even the faithfulness of God. How exquisitely this is illustrated in the

Savior's intercessory prayer for Peter, in the hour of his temptation and fall! Even though Peter denied his Lord, *Jesus was faithful.* He promised, ". . . I have prayed for you, that your faith *should not fail . . .*" (Luke 22:32).

## III. The Conquest of Temptation

". . . God is faithful, who will not allow you to be tempted beyond what you are able, but with the temptation will also make the way of escape, that you may be able to bear it" (10:13). The phrase, "the way of escape," is a vivid word in the original language. It means a way out of a defile (a long, narrow pass, as between mountains). The idea behind the expression is that of being surrounded by an army, and then suddenly seeing an escape route to safety. In terms of the Christian gospel, that way of escape is Jesus Christ our Lord. He who faced temptation and never succumbed; he who triumphed over every assault of Satan, is the One who can lead us into conquest. The secret is twofold:

### A. A Turning from Self

". . . God is faithful, who will not allow you to be tempted beyond what you are able, but with the temptation will also make the way of escape . . ." (10:13). In the moment of pressure we must recognize that in and of ourselves there is no hope. To imagine that we can stand in our own strength is to fail and ultimately fall. Like the apostle Paul, each of us must admit, ". . . I know that in me (that is, in my flesh) nothing good dwells; for to will is present with me, but how to perform what is good I do not find" (Rom. 7:18). On the other hand, there must be:

## B. A Turning to Christ

"... God ... will ... make the way of escape ..."
(10:13). In providing the Lord Jesus Christ there is no
need to fall to any temptation; there is a way out. It is
not the way of retreat, but the way of conquest in and
through Jesus Christ our victorious Lord. *Joseph* knew
this when he was given the courage to flee the seduc-
tive clutches of Potiphar's wife (see Gen. 39:12). *Moses*
knew this when he declined to be called the son of
Pharaoh's daughter, and chose to be identified with
the people of God (see Heb. 11:24–25); *Daniel* knew
this when he refused to be defiled with the food from
the king's table (see Dan. 1:8); *the New Testament
saints* throughout the ages have known the same victory. This is why Paul could exclaim, "... thanks be to
God who always leads us in triumph in Christ ..."
(2 Cor. 2:14).

### Illustration

A famous explorer in South America was once driven
back and forced to abandon his journey by an almost invis-
ible foe. He was equipped to meet jaguars, serpents, and
crocodiles. They proved to be no threat, but he had failed to
reckon with the LITTLE fellows—the millions of "chigoes"
better known as "chiggers." Today, watch the tiny things
which may spoil your testimony. Remember, "he that is
faithful in that which is least, is faithful also in much." Be
on guard against the "little foxes"—that evil thought, that
hasty word, that burst of temper, that snap judgment which
may bring defeat. Put on the whole armor of God by prayer,
Bible study, and spiritual exercise, and you will be able to
ward off enemies both large and small.[4]

## Conclusion

Are you under the pressure of life's temptations? There
is hope for you. Turn away from yourself and look to Jesus

who, under the greatest pressure anyone ever faced, endured the cross for you. As you consider him who suffered such contradiction of sinners against himself, do not give in to temptation, but give yourself over to Jesus, and victory will be yours.

# 10

# The Answer to Indecision
## *1 Kings 18:17–40*

"... How long will you falter between two opinions? If the LORD is God, follow Him; but if Baal, then follow him ..." (18:21).

## Introduction

When the rugged and fiery prophet Elijah challenged the people on Mount Carmel with the words, "... How long will you falter between two opinions? ..." (18:21), he was exposing the fundamental problem with the nation of Israel: its indecision and compromise, which resulted in moral, political and economic crises. Men and women were of two minds concerning the sovereignty and supremacy of God and, therefore, were suffering the inevitable doom of a divided house.

The historian Toynbee believes that the fall of the Roman Empire was due primarily to the loss of nerve on the part of the leading minority to make righteous decisions and then abide by them. This was true also of

Athens. The same can be said of our own day. We have lost the ability and courage to make righteous decisions. God is left out of our deliberations altogether. Behind the cloak of so called openmindedness, liberalism, and tolerance, we daily compromise the principles that exalt a nation. It is time, therefore, that we faced, personally and nationally, the great issue of Elijah's day: to follow God or Baal, and having made our decision to stand by it. As we think through the principles of this famous Old Testament narrative, observe that God's call to decision confronts men and women with:

## I. The Divine Alternative

". . . How long will you falter between two opinions? If the LORD is God, follow Him; but if Baal, then follow him . . ." (18:21). Elijah makes it quite plain that it is not only absurd, but impossible, for men and women to have two minds on this great question of Jehovah or Baal.

### A. There Was the Evidence for the True God

". . . If the LORD [Jehovah] is God, follow Him . . ." (18:21). Every Jew knew that Jehovah was the true God; the very name signified "the self-existent, eternal, almighty, and independent One." What is more, it was a common saying among the people that "Whoever can pronounce JEHOVAH is surely to be heard of God."

Then, of course, there were the inescapable associations of history with the name Jehovah. Elijah was careful to draw attention to this fact when he prayed, ". . . [Jehovah] LORD God of Abraham, Isaac, and Israel . . ." (18:36).

*Through Abraham* the Jewish people had learned of the God of resurrection; for it was supremely in Isaac that God had taught the lessons of death and resurrection (see Gen. 22; Heb. 11:19).

*Through Israel* the Jewish people had learned of the God of restoration, for it was supremely in Jacob (who became Israel) that God demonstrated his power to change lives (see Gen. 32).

In like manner, we know that Jehovah is the true God, for in an even greater sense we have seen the evidence of the God of revelation, resurrection, and restoration in the person and work of the Lord Jesus Christ.

### B. There Was the Evidence for the False God

". . . if Baal, then follow him . . ." (18:21). Baal was the god of man's creation and personified a subtle system of impure worship. As "the sun god," he was supposed to give man the freedom to do anything he liked under the sun; that is to say, he was a god of convenience, compromise, and corruption; or if you prefer, the deified projection of the self-life in its many subtle and evil forms.

Baal is still with us today; as a matter of fact, he reigns wherever God is dethroned in human life—however religious or pagan men and women might be.

We must face this divine alternative—". . . How long will we falter between two opinions? . . ." (18:21). How long are we going to limp back and forth like a lame man who cannot decide on which foot to settle? Is it to be God or Baal? We must decide. God calls us to a decision.

#### Illustration

When Gustavus Adolphus, king of Sweden, went over to Germany to help the Protestant princes in the cause of the Reformation, he was sorely tried by their lack of decision and lukewarmness. On meeting the ambassador of the Elector of Brandenburg, he uttered these stirring and memorable words: "This I say unto you plainly beforehand. I will hear and know nothing of neutrality. His Highness must be friend or foe. When I come to his border he must

declare himself hot or cold. The battle is between God
and the devil. Will his Highness hold with God? let him
stand at my side. Will he prefer to hold with the devil?
then he must fight against me. No third position will be
granted him."[1]

## II. The Divine Prerogative

Said Elijah to the people, ". . . the God who answers
by fire, He is God . . ." (18:24). The divine prerogative
would be demonstrated by an act from heaven which
only an all-powerful, all-holy, and all-loving God could
perform. The sign of the divine prerogative was to be
descending fire upon one or the other of the prepared
sacrifices.

First to perform were the followers of Baal. What a dra-
matic and vivid scene it must have been to watch those
450 prophets enter the contest! What pomp, color, sensu-
ality, fanaticism, self-mutilation, and noise; yet all to no
avail, for we read that ". . . there was no voice; no one
answered, no one paid attention" (18:29). Even the stab-
bing irony and contempt of Elijah failed to make them suc-
ceed. In fact, every fresh attempt to supplicate Baal only
served to reveal the utter emptiness, sham, and unreality of
manmade worship.

At last Elijah's turn came. He had waited until the
appointed hour of the evening sacrifice, and at God's com-
mand, in God's name, and for God's glory, he repaired the
altar of Jehovah and carefully prepared the sacrifice. Then
as an impressive safety measure, he called for twelve appli-
cations of water upon the sacrifice, until the trench around
the altar was full. This completed, Elijah reverently and
simply addressed God in prayer, requesting that the answer
from heaven would turn the hearts of the people back to
God (18:37). Verse 38 tells what happened: "Then the fire
of the LORD fell. . . ." In that fire the people saw:

## A. The Divine Prerogative of Power

".... the God who answers by fire, He is God ..."
(18:24). Here was a supernatural and miraculous act
which no one could deny. Only an Almighty God could
do this. God certainly revealed his power in answer to the
sacrifice on Mount Carmel; but even more did he reveal
his power on Mount Calvary. Never was there a death
accompanied by so many miraculous and supernatural
evidences as the death of the Lord Jesus. It is recorded
that ".... when the centurion and those with him, who
were guarding Jesus, saw the earthquake and the things
that had happened, they feared greatly, saying, 'Truly
this was the Son of God!'" (Matt. 27:54). If we want to be
convinced of the power of God we must come to Calvary and watch Jesus die. It will not be long before we
say with the centurion, "Truly this [is] the Son of God!"

## B. The Divine Prerogative of Justice

"Then the fire of the LORD fell and consumed the
burnt sacrifice, and the wood and the stones and the
dust, and it licked up the water that was in the trench"
(18:38). No one watched the fire that day without being
convinced of the holiness of God. Every person knew
that the altar and sacrifice were symbols of sin-bearing;
and to see God's fire utterly consume the sacrifice,
wood, stones, dust and water must have caused onlook-
ers to tremble at the thought of God's justice.

If we turn from Mount Carmel to Mount Calvary, we
see the same thing, only infinitely more terrible. When
Jesus was made sin for us, the fire of God's justice fell
with such a holy fierceness that he had to cry out,
".... My God, My God, why have You forsaken Me?"
(Matt. 27:46). Little wonder that the writer to the
Hebrews later contemplates the justice of God by remark-
ing, ".... our God is a consuming fire" (Heb. 12:29).

## C. The Divine Prerogative of Mercy

"Now when all the people saw it, they fell on their faces; and they said, 'The LORD, He is God! The LORD, He is God!'" (18:39). They knew that if they had received the punishment they deserved the fire would have fallen upon them and utterly consumed them; but because of God's goodness and mercy, the flame had been directed to the substitute sacrifice.

This is also the message of Calvary. If we had received the due reward of our sinful deeds, then the flame of God's justice would have fallen upon us. Instead, the fire of judgment has been exhausted on Jesus, our substitute and Savior, and we can therefore say, "Through the LORD's mercies we are not consumed . . ." (Lam. 3:22).

So with God's prerogative of power, justice, and mercy before us, the question is put to us, ". . . How long will we falter between two opinions? . . ." (18:21). Whom will we choose? Is it God or Baal? In the light of the cross we cannot remain neutral.

### Illustration

At the age of 16 George Mueller of Bristol, England was imprisoned for theft; and later at the university he lived a drinking, profligate life, acting dishonestly even toward his friends. Had he continued to pursue such a course of folly we might never have heard of him and he would have perished under God's condemnation. But at the age of 20 he came under the powerful influence of the Bible and he became a Christian. No longer was God's wrath and justice against him. In mercy, God transformed this thief into a new creature in Christ Jesus and he went on to become a giant in the earth in simplicity, faith, and obedience, and in breathtaking accomplishment through prayer and the Word.

## III. The Divine Imperative

Elijah insisted, ". . . If the LORD is God, follow Him . . ." (18:21). The divine imperative was nothing less than willingness to follow the Lord wholly and only. The story before us leaves us in no doubt as to what this following involved. It demanded:

### A. A Humble Repentance

A humble repentance on the part of the people; or the yielding of the mind to God. "... when all the people saw it, ... they said, 'The LORD, He is God!' ..." (18:39). There was to be no blind following. On the contrary, the following of God was to be the result of a clear revelation and a consequent change of mind.

We, too, will have to change our mind, and yield our mind, before we can confess that the LORD, He is God. Repentance is nothing less than a mind that takes sides with God against all that represents sin, self, and Satan; or in a word, Baal. How necessary it is that we take this first step of humble repentance. We must remember the words which came from the lips of the Lord Jesus, "... unless you repent you will ... likewise perish" (Luke 13:3).

### B. A Hearty Acceptance

A hearty acceptance on the part of the people; or the yielding of the heart to God. "... all the people ... fell on their faces ..." (18:39). No one who saw the fire fall that day and consume the sacrifice ever forgot it. A sense of awe, of reverence and acceptance filled his heart. Similarly, once we have been to Calvary, we can never be flippant or hesitant about following the Lord Jesus. The language of our hearts must surely be:

> Love so amazing, so divine,
> Demands my soul, my life, my all.
>
> Isaac Watts

Or, again, in the words of Frances R. Havergal:

> In full and glad surrender,
> I give myself to Thee,
> Thine utterly and only
> And evermore to be.

## C. A Holy Obedience

A holy obedience on the part of the people; or the yielding of the will to God. ". . . Seize the prophets of Baal! . . ." cried Elijah, ". . . Do not let one of them escape! . . ." (18:40). Elijah knew from the Word of God (see Deut. 13) that false prophets and anything else that would hinder the children of God from wholly following the Lord, must be slain. So he commanded that there should be no room for compromise, no tolerance of sin, evil and falsehood; all must be slain with the sword. Without a moment's delay the people obeyed and slaughtered the prophets of Baal until the Brook Kishon ran red with blood.

This is still the divine imperative. God still demands that sin must die, the old self-life must be finished with. The sword must be drawn against anything and everything that would prevent us from wholly following the Lord. Here, then, is decisive Christianity: a life that costs, but counts.

### Illustration

*Kamikaze* is the Japanese word for "divine wind." In the year 1281 God used a "divine wind," a typhoon to crush the invasion fleet mounted by an ambitious Mongol emperor in the wake of his conquest of China's Sung dynasty.

In World War II the retreating Japanese organized their own kamikaze suicide raids to take the wind out of the sails of the United States naval fleet. Altogether 1200 pilots slammed their bomb-laden planes—and themselves—into thirty-four American ships in the Pacific.

Today, we need "Christian kamikazes" who will take the faith anywhere the "divine wind" blows—regardless of the cost. Dietrich Bonhoeffer said, "When Christ calls a man, He bids him come and die."[2]

## Conclusion

What is our answer to God's call to decision? Remember that the divine alternative calls us to choose God; the divine prerogative calls us to prove God; and the divine imperative calls us to serve God. Is it God, or is it Baal? May your response be "Lord Jesus, in humble repentance, acceptance, and obedience, I come to Thee. Take my mind, my heart, my will. I will be 'ever, only, all for Thee.'"

# 11

# The Answer to Despair

## *Deuteronomy 33:26–29*

"The eternal God is your refuge, And underneath are the everlasting arms . . ." (33:27).

## Introduction

These words have been described as ". . . the blessing with which Moses the man of God blessed the children of Israel before his death" (33:1). They express one of the sublimest truths of faith that Moses had come to realize in the courts of Pharaoh, on the peak of Mount Sinai, in the hurry of the flight out of Egypt, and in the calm and glory of the divine presence. Moses had now finished his work on earth. He had given the Law, he had led the children of Israel, he had arrived in sight of Canaan. So God invited him up to Mount Nebo to see the land and then to die. As he faced his last enemy—death—Moses could say, "The eternal God is [my] refuge, And underneath are the everlasting arms . . ." (33:27). In that statement he affirmed his confidence in God. Millions of people since Moses have likewise found these words to be a source of comfort and consolation. Observe that:

## I. The Everlasting Arms Belong to the God of Eternity

"The eternal God is your refuge . . ." (33:27). In this materialistic age it sounds almost irrelevant, if not incomprehensible, to speak of eternity; yet man, in his search for meaning cannot avoid the fact of eternity. A British theologian, D. R. Davis, wrote a book titled *The World That We Have Forgotten.* In chapter after chapter he amassed material from church history, present human experience, and biblical doctrine to show that man in his quest for life is a creature of eternity. This is exactly what Moses is telling us here. Two thoughts need to be emphasized in this regard:

### A. The Eternal God Is the Answer to Life

"The eternal God is your refuge, And underneath are the everlasting arms . . ." (33:27). It matters not how depraved man may be; man is made for God (see Eccles. 3:11) and has a vast emptiness without him. This was illustrated in the 1960s. Young people, rebelling against our materialistic society, sought satisfaction in sex, drugs, music, Eastern mysticism and occultism, only to be disappointed. Then they turned on to Jesus in what was known as the "Jesus Revolution." These young people demonstrated a biblical principle: i.e., man was made for God; therefore, he is the creature of eternity.

An eminent Presbyterian clergyman once wrote: "I feel that if I can believe in God I believe in all that I need." When life is hard and all the allurements of synthetic and sophisticated living have ceased to attract, only one thing really matters: that is the God of eternity.

**Illustration**

Nearly everyone has heard the name of Helen Keller (1880–1968), American writer and lecturer, who was blind and deaf from infancy. At the age of nine her family secured a teacher who attempted to establish communication with her—without too much success. On a summer's day, her instructor took Helen to the pump and let water flow over her hand, and then tapped out on her palm "water." Helen grasped the message and was beside herself with joy that at last an idea had been conveyed to her by another person. Now that her curiosity had been aroused she made swift progress in her lessons, learning much about the world she could feel but could not see or hear.

Up to that point no one had been able to tell her about God, that he existed and cared for her. So her parents, who were Christians, engaged one of the greatest preachers in America at the time, Phillips Brooks, to communicate this truth to her through her tutor. Her response was remarkable. Though she had never heard a word from the outside world about such a Being she spoke up and said, ". . . I have been wishing for quite awhile that someone would talk to me about Him. I have been thinking about Him for a long time!" Deep within her soul God had instinctively planted the knowledge of himself. God can be known. He is ". . . the true Light which gives light to every man who comes into the world" (John 1:9).

## B. The Eternal God Is the Answer to Death

"The eternal God is your refuge . . ." (33:27). As we said earlier, Moses was facing death. God was about to bury him in a secret place that to this day has never been discovered or excavated. In light of his approaching death he could say, "The eternal God is [my] refuge . . ." (33:27).

Death is inevitable to all (see Heb. 9:27). Visit a cemetery and you'll find every age represented on the inscribed tombstones. Life is but a mist which appears for a moment and then vanishes away (see James 4:14).

This is because we are basically creatures of eternity. Life really begins when we have passed through ". . . the valley of the shadow of death" (Ps. 23:4). The question arises as to whether or not the eternal God is our refuge; whether we are in the everlasting arms of the God of eternity.

### Illustration

A little boy was offered the opportunity to select a dog for his birthday present. At the pet store, he was shown a number of puppies. From them he picked one whose tail was wagging furiously. When he was asked why he selected that particular dog, the little boy said, "I wanted the one with the happy ending." If we want to reach out for a life with a happy ending, we have no choice but to accept the living Christ as our Lord and Savior, follow him daily, and rejoice in the eternal life that awaits us.[1]

## II. The Everlasting Arms Belong to the God of Security

"The eternal God is your *refuge* . . ." (33:27). The word *refuge* is better rendered "dwelling place." The children of Israel needed to be reminded that though they were homeless and their national future was uncertain and hidden, yet they were in the presence and security of the eternal God. Ultimately, this is the only thing that matters; outside of this refuge the world is an empty, lonely, and homeless place. That is why the everlasting arms of God give such security.

### A. God Gives Security in the Place of Emptiness

"The eternal God is your refuge . . ." (33:27). Carl Gustav Jung, the Swiss psychiatrist and founder of the school of analytical psychology, has stated that "the central neurosis of our time is a sense of emptiness." Things may satisfy our bodies, and people may satisfy our souls, but only God can satisfy our spirits. Without God as our dwelling place and refuge, life is unspeakably empty. This is why people seek to drown their sorrows in business, pleasure, drugs, alcohol, or, as a last resort, death. When sickness and weakness overwhelm a person this sense of emptiness is heightened—unless he has a refuge to which he can escape. The true refuge is God himself. He is the dwelling place, the refuge of ineffable rest and peace.

### B. God Gives Security in the Place of Loneliness

"The eternal God is your refuge . . ." (33:27). Next to emptiness is the sense of loneliness which comes in life and in the hour of death. Moses, alone on that mountaintop, would have experienced utter dereliction had he not been able to say from the depths of his soul, "The eternal God is [my] refuge . . ." (33:27).

Just as the divine "dwelling place" answers to emptiness, so it does to loneliness. Modern man, whether young or old, seeks to escape from the haunting loneliness which pursues him night and day. Even in a crowded city, a busy office, or among members of his family, he can experience indescribable loneliness. But God is a refuge to such. The Bible says, "in Your presence is fullness of joy; At Your right hand are pleasures forevermore" (Ps. 16:11). No fellowship or friendship can equal communion with God.

### C. God Gives Security in the Place of Homelessness

"The eternal God is your refuge . . ." (33:27). For nearly forty years the children of Israel wandered in the wilderness without any permanent dwelling; yet, in the midst of it all, God proved to be their dwelling place and refuge. The home speaks of security from outside pressures. It is the place of understanding and love, the place of shelter, food, and rest. All this and more is God to those who trust him.

When Moses declared, "The eternal God is your refuge . . ." (33:27), he was affirming a precious fact based on personal experience. The eternal God had been his refuge. He had known better than most men the extremes of wealth and poverty, of power, and weakness, of fullness and want. He had known solitude amid the pleasures and glories of Pharaoh's court, but he had also enjoyed the divine society on the solitary slopes of Mount Horeb. He knew what Pharaoh could do for him, but he also knew what God could do for him. So he exclaims, "The eternal God is [my] refuge, And underneath are the everlasting arms . . ." (33:27). For Moses, God was his security.

**Illustration**

Charles Schultz, creator of the comic strip "Peanuts," pictures one of his characters, Linus, tenaciously clinging to his security blanket. Wherever he goes or whatever he does, Linus must have his blanket; he feels insecure without it. This may be humorous, but actually all of us have to have our security blankets of one kind or another. "The eternal God is your refuge, And underneath are the everlasting arms" (Deut. 33:27).[2]

## III. The Everlasting Arms Belong to the God of Ability

". . . underneath are the everlasting arms . . ." (33:27). Here we reach the climax of our text. Here we have a message for young and old alike. The basic thought behind this idea of the everlasting arms is that of strength, support, or ability. Whenever the hands or arms of God are referred to in Scripture they symbolize his ability in action. Think of:

## A. The Extent of Those Everlasting Arms

". . . underneath are the everlasting arms . . ." (33:27).
The word *underneath* in the Bible is used only this one
time. It is therefore a term big with meaning and sug-
gestiveness; or, as someone has pointed out, "It is the
index to a whole system of philosophical and theological thought."

Even in the world of science this concept of the
undergirding arms of God is wonderful to contemplate.
It has been said that the great contribution of science to
the sum of modern belief has been that underneath all
phenomena is that which is everlasting. Throughout the
centuries scientists have split the rocks, penetrated
space, plumbed the hidden depths of the earth and
looked into the secrets of nature in an attempt to understand the mystery of the universe, only to discover that
everything holds together and rests upon that which is
eternal; in other words, *the everlasting arms.*

When we come to personal experience, this truth
shines even brighter. There are three "d's" which sum
up the tragedy of human experience, but underneath
them all are the everlasting arms. There is the "d" of
*defeat.* Because man is ". . . brought forth in iniquity,
And in sin . . ." (Ps. 51:5) he is subject to defeat at every
point in his life. He is no match for the world, the flesh,
or the devil. The enemy of his soul is out to damn him;
but even at the deepest level of defeat ". . . underneath
are the everlasting arms . . ." (33:27).

There is also the "d" of *distress.* No one can know
defeat without experiencing distress. Sorrow can weigh
us down until we feel we can never rise again. Such
distress may lead eventually to depression. Spurgeon
once said, "I suppose some brethren have neither much
elevation or much depression. I could almost wish to
share their peaceful life, for I am much tossed up and
down; and although my joy is greater than that of most
men, my depression of spirit is such as few can have

any idea of. This week has been in some respects the crowning week of my life, but it closed with a horror of a great darkness, of which I will say no more than this—I bless God that at my worst, underneath me I found the everlasting arms."[3] Illness and weakness can bring on depression—especially when accentuated by certain medications—but even in circumstances like this we can say with Spurgeon, "underneath are the everlasting arms."

There is also the "d" of *despair* when death seems inevitable and all hope is gone. What can the world offer in such moments as these? What can atheists say, or those who scorn the gospel of Christ? In such an hour the Spirit of God can whisper, "Underneath are the everlasting arms." The extent of those arms meets us at the level of our greatest need.

### B. The Embrace of Those Everlasting Arms

". . . underneath are the everlasting arms . . ." (33:27). Those arms were outstretched on Calvary's cross to demonstrate that God was saying to men and women that whosoever will may come (see Rev. 22:17). Beginning in Genesis and working our way through to Revelation, we could find appropriate verses that speak of the arms of God. Nothing, however, excels the story of the father and his prodigal son. You will remember that when ". . . he was still a great way off, his father saw him and had compassion, and ran and fell on his neck and kissed him. And . . . said . . . Bring out the best robe and put it on him, and put a ring on his hand and sandals on his feet. And bring the fatted calf here and kill it, and let us eat and be merry" (Luke 15:20–24). In the embrace of those arms there was, first of all, *the forgiveness of the father*—He ". . . had compassion, and ran and fell on his neck and kissed him" (Luke 15:20). No words could better spell out the forgiving love of God. It matters not what far country you have wandered to, or what may have been the manner of riotous living, the everlasting arms are waiting to receive you.

In the embrace of those arms was also *the fellowship of the father*—". . . Bring out the best robe and put it on him, and put a ring on his hand and sandals on his feet" (Luke 15:22). This certainly suggests reinstatement and fellowship within the family home. When God puts his arms around you, you're in! What a message to a generation that is torn by racism, prejudice, and anti-socialism! You may not get a welcome anywhere else, but where there are open arms to receive you they are the arms of God, as revealed in Christ; they are the arms that were scarred on Calvary's cross.

Notice again that in the embrace of those arms is *the fullness of the father*—". . . bring the fatted calf here and kill it, and let us eat and be merry" (Luke 15:23). Every blessing which God has offered in the Lord Jesus Christ is included in the embrace of those arms. Paul could say, ". . . God . . . has blessed us with every spiritual blessing in the heavenly places in Christ" (Eph. 1:3). What comfort and consolation that brings to our souls! It matters not what our need may be: Jesus is adequate! In him alone we are complete (see Col. 2:10). Once we are in those arms we are safe forever.

### Illustration

A busy mother once overheard her two young daughters talking. One asked the other, "How do you know you are safe?" "Because I am holding Jesus tight with both my hands," replied the sister. "That is not safe," said the other, "suppose the devil came along and cut off your two hands?" The little sister was momentarily troubled, then her face suddenly beamed with joy. "Oh, I forgot! Jesus is holding me, and Satan couldn't cut off his hands, so I am safe!" This little girl had grasped the meaning of our Savior's words, ". . . I give them [my sheep] eternal life, and they shall never perish; neither shall anyone snatch them out of My hand" (John 10:28).

## Conclusion

How true are the words, ". . . underneath are the ever-lasting arms . . ." (33:27). Fanny J. Crosby, who became blind at six weeks of age, proved the reality of this truth when she wrote:

> Safe in the arms of Jesus,
> Safe from corroding care,
> Safe from the world's temptations,
> Sin cannot harm me there.
> Free from the blight of sorrow,
> Free from my doubts and fears;
> Only a few more trials,
> Only a few more tears.

> Jesus, my heart's dear refuge,
> Jesus has died for me;
> Firm on the Rock of Ages,
> Ever my trust shall be.
> Here let me wait with patience,
> Wait till the night is o'er;
> Wait till I see the morning
> Break on the golden shore.

# 12

# The Answer to Death

## Hebrews 9:24–28

". . . it is appointed for men to die once, but after this the judgment" (9:27).

## Introduction

Unlike other books, the Bible leaves us in no doubt as to the ultimate issues of life. No one can read through its pages without being absolutely sure about God, man, sin, and death. It is the only Book in the world which tells us where we have come from, where we are, and where we are going. Only people who adopt an ostrich-like attitude to life refuse to read and study the pages of Holy Scripture concerning a subject like death. They make excuses on the basis that such a theme is morbid, introspective, and pessimistic; but the fact remains that death is inescapable (9:27). Every man has an *appointment with death*. The passage before us speaks of:

## I. The Certainty of Death

". . . it is appointed for men to die once . . ." (9:27). There is a fig tree in India whose branches grow to a certain height, then begin to bend and grow downward to the ground. This tree is a symbol of human life: from the dust we came and to the dust we return. In other words:

### A. Death Is Inevitable

". . . it is appointed for men to die once . . ." (9:27). The psalmist asks, "What man can live and not see death? Can he deliver his life from the power of the grave?" (Ps. 89:48); and Solomon adds, "No one has power over the spirit to retain the spirit, And no one has power in the day of death. There is no discharge in that war, And wickedness will not deliver those who are given to it" (Eccles. 8:8). As soon as a baby is born war is declared on death. Even though the battle may rage for seventy years or more, there is no discharge in that war. Death fights on until it has claimed its victim. Only two men in the Bible never died—Enoch and Elijah; but that does not affect the fact that ". . . it is appointed for men to die once, but after this the judgment" (9:27).

### B. Death Is Impartial

". . . it is appointed for men to die once . . ." (9:27). Death is like the mailman who comes to the homes of the rich and the poor, and delivers to one man a wedding invitation, and to his neighbor the sad news of a friend's decease; to one the pleasant news that his ship has arrived in port, and to the other news of disaster and bankruptcy. Death is no respecter of persons, position, or age. Paul sums it up when he says, "Therefore, just as through one man sin entered the world, and death through sin, . . . thus death spread to all men, because all sinned" (Rom. 5:12).

### Illustration

Some time ago a newspaper reported the death of a woman on whom the world had lavished its choicest gifts. She came from a wealthy, distinguished family, and in each of two marriages she became the wife of a man prominent in the service of the country. A president of the United States attended her first marriage. Her beauty was such that her portrait was done by a famous American painter. Her wealth permitted her to buy the jewels of a princess. The obituary, however, said nothing about the unending life to which she has now gone. Nor did it say a word about her preparation—if any—for that life. Riches, beauty, interests, fame—all these she was forced to leave behind at the moment of death, for in the last analysis, death is not only inevitable, but impartial.

## II. The Consequences of Death

". . . it is appointed for men to die once, but after this the judgment" (9:27). It is clear from the teaching of Holy Scripture that death is not the end of life, but rather a change of life; or to put it in another form, death is but the doorway to an afterlife. What determines the eternal destiny of a man or a woman after death is the day of judgment. To get rid of the doctrine of judgment a man must plunge into the gloomy absurdities of atheism, and he cannot be safe there for he still has his conscience left. No man who has any sense of justice can believe that wrong will forever go unpunished. He has a premonition that after death he must face the judge of all the earth. The Bible says that God ". . . has appointed a day on which He will judge the world in righteousness by the Man whom He has ordained . . ." (Acts 17:31). Notice carefully from this amazing statement that:

## A. The Period for the Judgment Has Been Ordered Already

God ". . . has appointed a day . . ." (Acts 17:31). No one can read the Bible without being impressed with God's strange work of judgment. If God in times past has not spared angels, archangels, and even his only Son, [when He ". . . bore our sins in His own body on the tree . . ." (1 Peter 2:24)] will he spare you? As Peter puts it, ". . . If the righteous one is scarcely saved, where will the ungodly and the sinner appear?" (1 Peter 4:18).

## B. The Person for the Judgment Has Been Ordained Already

God ". . . has appointed a day on which He will judge the world in righteousness by the Man whom He has ordained . . ." (Acts 17:31). During his ministry here on earth Jesus made it clear that ". . . the Father . . . has committed all judgment to the Son" (John 5:22). This means that the one who now stands at the door of your heart as Savior, seeking an entrance, will one day be your judge, if rejected.

## C. The Proof for the Judgment Has Been Offered Already

". . . because He has appointed a day on which He will judge the world in righteousness by the Man whom He has ordained. He has given assurance of this to all, by raising Him from the dead" (Acts 17:31). The fact that Jesus Christ lives today is God's infallible proof that he will judge men and women on the "appointed day." You see, God is ". . . of purer eyes than to behold evil, And cannot look on wickedness . . ." (Heb. 1:13). He must therefore judge sin at the cross now, or at the throne in the final day of reckoning. We sing so lustily, "He lives, He lives . . . ," but we often fail to realize that his resurrection and present session are proof that the adorable Savior will be the awesome judge at the judgment seat—for believers, and the great white throne—for the unsaved.

So we see that when a person slumps in his chair because of a heart attack, or is knocked down by an automobile, or is stabbed on some dark street by a hoodlum, that is not the end. He does not just pass away like an animal. On the contrary, he enters another dimension of life where he has to stand before the judgment throne of God in order to determine his eternal destiny. ". . . it is appointed for men to die once, but after this the judgment" (9:27).

### Illustration

Burt Olney was a skeptic. When a young minister was called to a local church, Burt attended just for the purpose of criticizing and arguing with the new pastor. After the service he said to the man of God: "You did well, but you know, I don't believe in the infallibility of your Bible." "It is appointed unto men once to die, but after this the judgment," was the young preacher's calm assertion. "I can prove to you that there is no such thing as judgment after death," declared the skeptic. "But men do die," the young pastor continued, "For it is appointed unto men once to die, but after this the judgment." "But that's no argument, man," the skeptic protested, "Let's get down to business and discuss this matter in regular argument form." The young clergyman shook his head, "I am here to preach the Word of God, and not to argue over it." Burt Olney was greatly annoyed and turned away with the remark, "I don't believe you know enough about your Bible to argue about it anyway." "Perhaps you are right," was the calm reply, "but just remember this, sir, 'It is appointed unto men once to die, but after this the judgment.'" Burt Olney left for home but the very tree toads along the way seemed to sing the awful verse in his ear. The stream he crossed and the frogs in the pond seemed to croak, "Judg-ment, Judg-ment!" The next morning Burt called at the parsonage. "I have come to see you about that verse of Scripture you gave me last night," he said. "I spent a terrible time since then. These words have burned their way into me. Tell me, what must I do to be saved? I've got to get rid of this torture." The Scripture was opened to him and Burt Olney, through faith in the finished work of Christ, became a new creature.[1]

## III. The Conquest of Death

". . . so Christ was offered once to bear the sins of many. To those who eagerly wait for Him He will appear a second time, apart from sin, for salvation" (9:28). Because sin has entered into the world, resulting in death for all the human race, God sent his Son to die on Calvary's cross so that he might bear the sins of many and provide a salvation from:

### A. The Cause of Death

We read that the Lord Jesus became flesh and blood that ". . . through death He might destroy him who had the power of death, that is, the devil" (Heb. 2:14). It was Satan who introduced death into God's fair creation. This is why he is described as having ". . . the power of death . . ." (Heb. 2:14). But the Lord Jesus entered human history to ". . . destroy the works of the devil" (1 John 3:8). Like David, who decapitated Goliath with his own sword, our Lord Jesus Christ struck the devil a mortal blow with his own weapon of death. The devil, therefore, has no power over the children of God in respect of death. To the Christian, death is but a sleep from which he awakens to enjoy forever the glorious presence of his Lord and Savior.

### B. The Sting of Death

Paul reminds us that "The sting of death is sin . . ." and then adds, "O Death, where is your sting? O Hades, where is your victory? . . . But thanks be to God, who gives us the victory through our Lord Jesus Christ" (1 Cor. 15:55–57). Because Jesus has taken the sting into his own body, all of us who believe in him will never have to stand before the great white throne of judgment. For us the sting of death is gone.

### Illustration

A mother was hanging up wash in the yard while her little girl was playing on the grass. Suddenly the child jumped to her feet, crying, "Mamma, Mamma, a wasp! a wasp!" "Run into your mother's arms," commanded the mother. The little girl did just that, and all was still for a moment. The mother quietly assured her daughter that all was well. "The wasp will not sting you now." "Why?" asked the child. "Look," said the mother, showing her arm, "I have taken the sting for you."

## C. The Fear of Death

Through the cross Jesus has effected a deliverance for ". . . those who through fear of death were all their lifetime subject to bondage" (Heb. 2:15). The saints of the Old Testament could sing, ". . . though I walk through the valley of the shadow of death, I will fear no evil . . ." (Ps. 23:4); and the saints of the New Testament can join with Paul in exclaiming, ". . . I am hard pressed between the two, having a desire to depart and be with Christ, which is far better" (Phil. 1:23). To such, death holds no terror, but rather affords a glorious anticipation of release from the limitations of this earthly life into the liberation of the heavenly life. Indeed, in one of his figures of speech Paul describes death as "the lifting of the anchor" of a straitened life, in order to begin the voyage of the fuller life across the uncharted seas of eternity. Whitman called it: "Cool-enfolding death"; Ingersoll, "the fine serenity of death"; Shakespeare, "A necessary end." How different are the words of Scripture—". . . to die is gain" (Phil. 1:21).

**Illustration**

An Oriental girl of 17 years was dying of tuberculosis in an American hospital. As death's cold fingers touched her she screamed with fear. Her Buddha seemed indifferent to her fear. The nurses had no medicine that would quiet her troubled heart. A missionary talked with her about Jesus. Over and over she read, "He that believeth on the SON hath life." She closed her tired eyes and prayed. Then as she counted the words out on her thin fingers she whispered, "The Lord is my Savior." The missionary was about to leave, but her plea arrested him—"Oh, don't go, tell me more about Jesus." He told her more and she drank in every word. She spent her waking hours reading John's Gospel. The next day he saw her again and told her of the place Jesus had prepared for her. "Are you afraid to die?" "No, the fear is all gone, I am ready to die." Early the next day her weary eyes closed, her tired heart stopped and she slipped away into His everlasting arms.[2]

## Conclusion

Are we prepared to meet God? Remember the certainty of death: we cannot escape it for it is inevitable and impartial. There is a solemn consequence about death: it ushers us into the presence of God before whom we have to answer for our words and our works here upon earth. Thank God, there is a conquest of death which the Lord Jesus Christ has effected through his own redemptive sacrifice on Calvary's cross. To know him personally is to be delivered from the very cause, sting, and fear of death. We must trust him now so that we can say with the psalmist, ". . . though I walk through the valley of the shadow of death, I will fear no evil . . ." (Ps. 23:4).

# Endnotes

## Introduction

1. E. P. Alldredge, *101 Expository Sermon Outlines* (Nashville: Broadman, 1942). Adapted by *Pulpit Helps,* vol. 5, no. 5, published by AMG International, Chattanooga, Tenn. 37422.

## Chapter 1

1. Richard Chenevix Trench, quoted in Walter B. Knight, *Knight's Master Book of New Illustrations* (Grand Rapids: Eerdmans, 1956), p. 484.
2. W. J. Hart, in Paul Lee Tan, *Encyclopedia of 7,700 Illustrations* (Garland, Tex.: Bible Communications, 1979), p. 1035.
3. V. Raymond Edman in *Today,* vol. 30, no. 1 (Palos Heights, Ill.: The Back to God Hour, Feb. 1, 1980).
4. Henry G. Bosch, *Our Daily Bread* (Grand Rapids: Radio Bible Class, Jan. 12, 1974).
5. Ibid., June 12, 1974, adapted.

## Chapter 2

1. *The Prairie Overcomer,* quoted in Paul Lee Tan, *Encyclopedia of 7,700 Illustrations* (Garland, Tex.: Bible Communications, 1979), p. 1247.
2. *Evangelistic Illustration,* ibid., 495.

## Chapter 3

1. V. Raymond Edman, *Wheaton College Bulletin* (Wheaton, Ill.: Wheaton College, n.d.).

2. *Evangelistic Illustration,* quoted in Paul Lee Tan, *Encyclopedia of 7,700 Illustrations* (Garland, Tex.: Bible Communications, 1979), p. 435, adapted.

## Chapter 4

1. A. Naismith, *1,200 Notes, Quotes, and Anecdotes* (Hammersmith: Pickering & Inglis, 1963), p. 203, adapted.
2. Henry G. Bosch, *Our Daily Bread* (Grand Rapids: Radio Bible Class, n.d.).
3. John R. W. Stott, *The Epistles of John,* Tyndale New Testament Commentaries (Grand Rapids: Eerdmans, 1979). p. 63.

## Chapter 5

1. Donald N. Paulson, "How to Deal with Your Loneliness," *The Watchman-Examiner* (Aug. 8, 1968), p. 494.
2. Ray O. Jones, quoted in Paul Lee Tan, *Encyclopedia of 7,700 Illustrations* (Garland, Tex.: Bible Communications, 1979), p. 1380.
3. *Gospel Herald,* ibid., 1379.
4. C. I. Scofield, ibid., 1267.
5. *Indian Christian,* quoted in A. Naismith, *1,200 Notes, Quotes, and Anecdotes* (Hammersmith: Pickering & Inglis, 1963), p. 183-84.
6. Henry G. Bosch, *Our Daily Bread* (Grand Rapids: Radio Bible Class, June 30, 1984).
7. Walter B. Knight, *3,000 Illustrations for Christian Service* (Grand Rapids: Eerdmans, 1952), p. 78.

## Chapter 6

1. Alexander Maclaren, *Expositions of Holy Scripture,* vol. 16 (Grand Rapids: Eerdmans, 1959), p. 119.
2. *Day by Day with Jesus* (St. Louis: Concordia, 1979).

## Chapter 7

1. B. W. Woods, *Understanding Suffering* (Grand Rapids: Baker, 1974), pp. 74-75.

## Chapter 8

1. Paul Lee Tan, *Encyclopedia of 7,700 Illustrations* (Garland, Tex.: Bible Communications, 1979), p. 435.
2. *Day by Day with Jesus* (St. Louis: Concordia, 1979).

## Chapter 9

1. Warren W. Wiersbe, *Listening to the Giants* (Grand Rapids: Baker, 1980), p. 346.
2. *Sermons Illustrated* (Holland, Ohio, April 28, 1987).

3. William Barclay, *The Revelation of John,* 2d ed., vol. 1 (Edinburgh: The Saint Andrew Press, n.d.), p. 144, adapted.

4. *Sermons Illustrated* (Holland, Ohio, July 26, 1986).

## Chapter 10

1. *Evangel Herald,* quoted in Walter B. Knight, *3,000 Illustrations for Christian Service* (Grand Rapids: Eerdmans, 1952), p. 118.

2. Adapted from *Sermons Illustrated* (Holland, Ohio, Nov. 17, 1986).

## Chapter 11

1. *Sermons Illustrated* (Holland, Ohio, Nov. 19, 1986).

2. Carl C. Williams, quoted in Paul Lee Tan, *Encyclopedia of 7,700 Illustrations* (Garland, Tex.: Bible Communications, 1979), p. 5249.

3. Charles H. Spurgeon, *The Great Texts of the Bible* (New York: Scribner, n.d.), p. 75.

## Chapter 12

1. *Our Daily Bread* (Grand Rapids: Radio Bible Class, April 17, 1959).

2. *Gospel Herald,* quoted in Walter B. Knight, *Knight's Master Book of New Illustrations* (Grand Rapids: Eerdmans, 1956), pp. 160-61.

# For Further Reading

## Chapter 1

Barclay, William. *Daily Study Bible* (Philippians, Colossians, and Thessalonians). Rev. ed. Philadelphia: Westminster Press, 1975–1976.

Eadie, John. *A Commentary on the Greek Text of the Epistle of Paul to the Philippians.* 1859. Reprint. Grand Rapids: Baker Book House, 1979.

Hawthorne, Gerald F. *Word Biblical Commentary* (Philippians). Vol. 43. Waco, Tex.: Word Books, 1983.

Ironside, H. A. *Notes on Philippians.* Neptune, N.J.: Loizeaux Brothers, Inc., 1922.

King, Guy. *Joy Way: An Expositional Application of the Epistle to the Philippians.* London: Marshall, Morgan & Scott, 1963.

Martin, Ralph. *The Epistle of Paul to the Philippians.* Grand Rapids: Wm. B. Eerdmans Publishing Co., 1978.

Meyer, F. B. *The Epistle to the Philippians.* Grand Rapids: Zondervan Publishing House, 1956.

Motyer, J. A. *Philippian Studies: The Richness of Christ.* Chicago: InterVarsity Press, 1966.

Moule, Handley C. G. *Philippian Studies: Lessons in Faith and Love from St. Paul's Epistle to the Philippians.* 1897. Reprint. Grand Rapids: Zondervan Publishing House, 1962.

Rees, Paul S. *The Adequate Man: Paul in Philippians.* Westwood, N.J.: Fleming H. Revell Co., 1959.

Robertson, A. T. *Paul's Joy in Christ: Studies in Philippians.* 1917. Reprint. Grand Rapids: Baker Book House, 1979.

Vine, W. E. *Epistles to the Philippians and Colossians.* London: Oliphants, Ltd., 1955.

Wuest, Kenneth S. *Philippians in the Greek New Testament.* Grand Rapids: Wm. B. Eerdmans Publishing Co., 1953.

## Chapter 2

Alexander, J. A. *Commentary on the Gospel of Mark.* Classic Commentary Library. 1864. Reprint. Grand Rapids: Zondervan Publishing House, 1955.

Cole, Robert A. *The Gospel According to St. Mark.* Tyndale New Testament Commentaries. Grand Rapids: Wm. B. Eerdmans Publishing Co., 1961.

English, E. Schuyler. *Studies in the Gospel According to Mark: A Comprehensive Exposition of the Gospel of the Servant-Son of God.* New York: Our Hope, 1943.

Ironside, H. A. *Expository Notes on the Gospel of Mark.* Neptune, N.J.: Loizeaux Brothers, Inc., 1948.

Ryle, J. C. *Expository Thoughts on the Gospel of Mark.* Carlisle, Pa.: Banner of Truth Trust, 1985.

Swete, Henry Barclay. *Commentary on Mark.* Grand Rapids: Kregel Publications, 1977.

Taylor, Vincent. *The Gospel According to St. Mark.* London: Macmillan Co., 1963.

## Chapters 3 and 6

Cochrane, Elvis E. *The Epistles of Peter.* Grand Rapids: Baker Book House, 1965.

Cramer, George H. *First and Second Peter.* Chicago: Moody Press, 1967.

Exell, Joseph S., ed. *The Biblical Illustrator on 1 Peter.* Grand Rapids: Baker Book House, 1978.

Hiebert, David E. *First Peter.* Chicago: Moody Press, 1984.

Rees, Paul S. *Triumphant in Trouble.* Westwood, N.J.:Fleming H. Revell Co., 1962.

Spence, H. D. M., and Joseph S. Exell, eds. *The Pulpit Commentary (Epistles of Peter, John and Jude).* Vol. 22. Grand Rapids: Wm. B. Eerdmans Publishing Co., 1950.

Stibbs, Alan. *First Epistle of Peter.* Tyndale New Testament Commentaries. Grand Rapids: Wm. B. Eerdmans Publishing Co., 1960.

Thomas, W. Griffith. *The Apostle Peter: Outline Studies.* Grand Rapids: Wm. B. Eerdmans Publishing Co., 1956.

Wuest, Kenneth S., *First Peter in the Greek New Testament.* Grand Rapids: Wm. B. Eerdmans Publishing Co., 1942.

## Chapters 4 and 8

Bruce, F. F. *The Epistles of John.* Grand Rapids: Wm. B. Eerdmans Publishing Co., 1983.

Candlish, Robert Smith. *The First Epistle of John.* Grand Rapids: Kregel Publications, 1979.

King, Guy. *The Fellowship: An Expositional and Devotional Study of 1 John.* London: Marshall, Morgan & Scott, 1954.

Law, Robert. *The Tests of Life: A Study of the First Epistle of St. John.* 3rd. ed. 1914. Reprint. Grand Rapids: Baker Book House, 1978.

Lias, John J. *An Exposition of the First Epistle of John.* Minneapolis: Klock and Klock Christian Publishers, 1982.

Morgan, James, and Samuel Cox. *The Epistles of John.* Minneapolis: Klock and Klock Christian Publishers, 1982.

Stedman, Ray C. *Expository Studies in 1 John: Life by the Son.* Waco, Tex.: Word Inc., 1980.

Stott, John R. W. *The Epistles of John.* Tyndale New Testament Commentary. Grand Rapids: Wm. B. Eerdmans Publishing Co., 1979.

Strauss, Lehman. *The Epistles of John.* New York: Loizeaux Brothers, Inc., 1962.

Vine, W. E. *The First Epistle of John.* Grand Rapids: Zondervan Publishing House, 1965.

## Chapter 5

Alexander, Joseph Addison. *The Psalms Translated and Explained.* 1864. Reprint. Grand Rapids: Zondervan Publishing House.

Delitzsch, Franz. *Biblical Commentary on the Psalms.* Trans. Francis Bolton. 3 vols. Grand Rapids: Wm. B. Eerdmans Publishing Company, 1949.

Dickson, David. *A Commentary on the Psalms.* 2 vols. Minneapolis: Klock and Klock Christian Publishers, 1980.

Ironside, H. A. *Studies on Psalms: Book One.* Neptune, N.J.: Loizeaux Brothers, Inc, 1952.

Kidner, Derek. *Psalms: An Introduction and Commentary on Books I and II.* Tyndale Old Testament Commentaries. Downers Grove, Ill.: InterVarsity Press, 1973.

Klug, Ron. *Psalms: A Guide to Prayer & Praise.* Fisherman Bible Studyguide Series. Wheaton, Ill.: Harold Shaw Publishers, 1979.

Maclaren, Alexander. *The Psalms.* 3 vols. Minneapolis: Klock and Klock Christian Publishers, 1980.

Morgan, G. Campbell. *Notes on the Psalms.* New York: Fleming H. Revell Co., 1947.

Patterson, John. *The Praises of Israel.* Totowa, N.J.: Charles Scribner's Sons, 1950.

Scroggie, W. Graham. *Know Your Bible* (The Psalms). Vols. 1–4. New York: Fleming H. Revell Co., 1948.

Spurgeon, Charles. *The Treasury of David.* 6 vols. Grand Rapids: Zondervan Publishing House, 1963.

Terrien, Samuel. *The Psalms and their Meaning for Today.* New York: The Bobbs-Merrill Co., 1952.

Walker, H. Rollin. *The Modern Message of the Psalms.* Nashville: Abingdon Press, 1938.

Weiser, Artur. *The Psalms: A Commentary.* Translated from the German. London: SCM Press, 1962.

## Chapter 7

Barclay, William. *Daily Study Bible* (The Letters to the Corinthians). Rev. ed. Philadelphia: Westminster Press, 1975–1976.

Barrett, Charles Kingsley. *A Commentary on the Second Epistle to the Corinthians.* Harper's New Testament Commentaries. New York: Harper and Row, 1973.

Hodge, Charles. *An Exposition of the Second Epistle to the Corinthians.* Grand Rapids: Baker Book House, 1980.

Kent, Homer Austin, Jr. *A Heart Opened Wide: Studies in II Corinthians.* New Testament Studies. Grand Rapids: Baker Book House, 1982.

Morgan, G. Campbell. *The Corinthian Letters of Paul: An Exposition of I and II Corinthians.* Westwood, N.J.: Fleming H. Revell Co., 1956.

Moule, Handley. *The Second Epistle to the Corinthians: A Translation, Paraphrase, and Exposition.* Ed. A. W. Handley Moule. London: Pickering & Inglis, 1962.

Redpath, Alan. *Blessings Out of Buffetings: Studies in II Corinthians.* Westwood, N.J.: Fleming H. Revell Co., 1962.

Stedman, Ray C. *Expository Studies in 2 Corinthians: Power Out of Weakness.* Waco, Tex.: Word Books, 1982.

## Chapter 9

Barclay, William. *Daily Study Bible* (The Letters to the Corinthians). Rev. ed. Philadelphia: Westminster Press, 1975–1976.

Godet, F. *Commentary on the First Epistle of Paul to the Corinthians.* Grand Rapids: Zondervan Publishing House, 1957.

Hodge, Charles. *An Exposition of the First Epistle to the Corinthians.* 1857. Reprint. Grand Rapids: Wm. B. Eerdmans Publishing Co., 1956.

Morgan, G. Campbell. *The Corinthian Letters of Paul: An Exposition of I and II Corinthians.* New York: Fleming H. Revell Co., 1946.

Vine, W. E. *I Corinthians.* Grand Rapids: Zondervan Publishing House, 1961.

## Chapter 10

Cambridge Bible for Schools and Colleges. Cambridge: Cambridge University, 1884–1899.

Devotional Commentary. London: Religious Tract Society, 1905–1931.

Expositor's Bible. 1888–1905. Reprint. Grand Rapids: Wm B. Eerdmans Publishing Co., 1943.

Farrar, Frederick William. *The First Book of Kings.* Minneapolis: Klock and Klock Christian Publishers, 1981.

Kaiser, Walter C. Jr. *Have You Seen the Power of God Lately: Lessons for Today from Elijah.* San Bernardino, Calif.: Here's Life Publishers, Inc., 1987.

Krummacher, Frederick W. *Elijah the Tishbite.* Grand Rapids: Zondervan Publishing House, n.d.

MacDuff, John Ross. *Elijah, the Prophet of Fire.* Minneapolis: Klock and Klock Christian Publishers, 1982.

Meyer, F. B. *Elijah: And the Secret of His Power*. London: Marshall, Morgan & Scott, 1954.

Pink, Arthur W. *The Life of Elijah*. Rev. ed. London: Banner of Truth Trust, 1963.

Taylor, William M. *Bible Biographies*. 8 vols. 1874–1891. Reprint (5 vols.). Grand Rapids: Baker Book House, 1961–1962.

Wood, Leon J. *Elijah: Prophet of God*. Des Plaines, Ill.: Regular Baptist, 1968.

Whyte, Alexander. *Bible Characters*. Edinburgh: Oliphants, Ltd., 3:93.

## Chapter 11

Craigie, P. C. *New International Commentary on the Old Testament*. Grand Rapids: Wm. B. Eerdmans Publishing Co., 1976.

Mackintosh, Charles Henry. *Genesis to Deuteronomy: Notes on the Pentateuch*. 6 vols. 1880–1882. Reprint (1 vol.. Neptune, N.J.: Loizeaux Brothers, Inc., 1972.

Schultz, Samuel J. *The Old Testament Speaks*. New York: Harper and Row, 1960.

## Chapter 12

Barclay, William. *Daily Study Bible* (Hebrews). Philadelphia: Westminster Press, 1975–1976.

Brown, John. *The Epistle to the Hebrews*. London: Banner of Truth Trust, 1961.

Bruce, F. F. *The Epistle to the Hebrews* (New International Commentary of the New Testament). Grand Rapids: Wm. B. Eerdmans Publishing Co., 1964.

DeHaan, M. R. *Hebrews*. Grand Rapids: Zondervan Publishing House, 1959.

Hughes, Philip Edgcumbe. *A Commentary on the Epistle to the Hebrews*. Grand Rapids: Wm. B. Eerdmans Publishing Co., 1977.

Ironside, H. A. *Studies in the Epistle to the Hebrews and the Epistle to Titus*. New York: Loizeaux Brothers, Inc., 1958.

Kent, Homer A., Jr. *The Epistle to the Hebrews: A Commentary*. Grand Rapids: Baker Book House, 1972.

Lang, G. H. *The Epistle to the Hebrews*. London: The Paternoster Press, 1951.

Macaulay, J. C. *Expository Commentary on Hebrews*. Chicago: Moody Press, 1978.

Meyer, F. B. *The Way Into the Holiest: Expositions of the Epistle to the Hebrews*. London: Marshall, Morgan & Scott, n.d.

Morgan, G. Campbell. *The Triumphs of Faith*. London: Pickering & Inglis, n.d.

Murray, Andrew. *The Holiest of All: An Exposition of the Epistle to the Hebrews*. New York: Fleming H. Revell Co., 1965.

Newell, William R. *Hebrews Verse by Verse*. Chicago: Moody Press, 1947.

Owen, John. *An Exposition of Hebrews*. Evansville, Ind.: Sovereign Grace Publishers, 1960.

Pink, Arthur W. *An Exposition of Hebrews*. 3 vols. Grand Rapids: Baker Book House, 1954.

Pfeiffer, Charles F. *The Epistle to the Hebrews*. Chicago: Moody Press, 1962.

Saphir, Adolph. *The Epistle to the Hebrews: An Exposition.* 2d ed. 2 vols. Reprint. Grand Rapids: Zondervan Publishing House, 1902.

Seiss, Joseph A. *Popular Lectures on the Epistle of Paul the Apostle to the Hebrews.* Reprint. *Lectures on Hebrews.* Grand Rapids: Baker Book House, 1954.

Thomas, W. H. Griffith. *Hebrews: A Devotional Commentary.* n.d. Reprint. Grand Rapids: Wm. B. Eerdmans Publishing Co., 1962.

Vine, W. E. *Hebrews.* London: Oliphants, Ltd., 1952.

Way, Arthur S. *Letters of St. Paul and Hebrews.* London: Macmillan & Co. Ltd., 1935.

Westcott, B. F. *The Epistle to the Hebrews: The Greek Text with Notes and Essays.* 3rd ed. 1903. Reprint. Grand Rapids: Wm. B. Eerdmans Publishing Co., 1955.

Wiersbe, Warren W. *Be Confident: An Expository Study of the Epistle to the Hebrews.* Wheaton, Ill.: Victor Books, 1982.

Wuest, Kenneth S. *Hebrews in the Greek New Testament for the English Reader.* Grand Rapids: Wm B. Eerdmans Publishing Co., 1947.